The Paranormal:

An Open-Minded Guide

By
C.C Cutts

Contents

My Thanks

Introduction: Introductionto the Open-Minded Guide

Chapter One: What is the paranormal?

Chapter Two: Old school equipment

Chapter Three: Modern day equipment

Chapter Four: Equipment Experiments

Chapter Five: Conducting an Investigation

Chapter Six: Investigation Ideas

Chapter Seven: Divination Techniques

Chapter Eight: Arguments for and Against Reported Paranormal Activity

Chapter Nine: Haunted and Cursed Artefacts

ChapterTen: Famous Ghosts

Chapter Eleven: Haunted Locations

Chapter Twelve: How to create a ghost

Chapter Thirteen: Explanations for Paranormal Activity

Chapter Fourteen: Faiths, Ghosts and Exorcisms

Chapter Fifteen: Paranormal Believers

Chapter Sixteen: Paranormal Sceptics

Chapter Seventeen: Fraudulent Paranormal

Chapter Eighteen: Famous Paranormal Debunking

Chapter Nineteen: Glossary of Paranormal Terms

Chapter Twenty: Final Thought

Bibliography, Source Materials and Useful Websites

My thanks

To my wonderful Princess, thank you for believing in me I will love you always and forever. You are my inspiration and my whole world.

To my wonderful family (No I will not give you royalties), thank you for helping me to become the man I am today, I love you all.

To my friends (No, I will not give you a free copy), thank you for being there when I needed you the most.

To those who I have worked with in the paranormal community (You saw this coming) thank you for the lessons you have taught me and for giving me a chance to explore the world of the paranormal.

Finally, thank you dear reader for purchasing this book. I truly hope you will enjoy reading it as much as I have writing it.

Introduction to the Open-Minded Guide

I can guarantee that, you the reader, picked up this book not because of whatever fancy cover has been added to it, but because it contained the word paranormal. Since time immemorial, we as a species have been fascinated with the 'paranormal', from the Mayan Calendar to Dracula's aversion to sunlight and even ghosts that make things go bump in the night.

From a young age I found myself fascinated by the unknown. The first time that I believed I saw a ghost was when I was six years old. One evening I walked downstairs to get a glass of water from the kitchen, I was paralysed with fear as I witnessed a white mass that moved from the bottom of the stairs and then ascended them. Was this just my imagination running wild? A tired mind? Or an apparition? I always felt like the house didn't want me to be there but whatever it was it started a lifetime obsession with the world of the paranormal. The next time I saw something I could not explain was when I was about fourteen, we had recently moved to a new house. My bedroom was downstairs and one night, I walked into the kitchen and when I looked towards the stairs, I saw another white figure, again moving from the bottom of the stairs and slowly ascending them. My mind raced with questions; what was it? Was it the same entity from the other house? Or was I just tired and my mind was playing tricks on me? After this sighting I never witnessed the white figure again by it was not to be the end of my experiences by far. Fast forward to my late teenage years, I moved into a house that had quite a history. During World War Two, the original house where mine now stood was destroyed during a German air raid. For the first few weeks after moving in every night between 10pm and 1am there would be the sound of air raid sirens. Could this have been residual energy that was created which was created when the energy from the bomb connected to the site? Or just a tired mind, confusing passing vehicles making sounds? Unfortunately, I would never find out, all I know is I wasn't the only one in the house who heard the sound of the sirens.

All these experiences have definitely led me to some interesting places and meeting more interesting people. I met a wonderful woman who would eventually become my girlfriend, she is a witch and this in turn allowed me to interact with some wonderful people, this deepened my knowledge and understanding of magic and its place in the world. For a time, I also worked with alongside a medium who taught me about the world of ghost hunting and how to investigate it. This ultimately led to me discovering the other side of the paranormal; that of parapsychology.

Parapsychology is the study of alleged psychic phenomena and other claims such as near-death experiences. Parapsychology is an eye-opening subject; it makes you look at unexplained phenomena in more depth to see if you can find a logical explanation for any activity you may encounter.

In this book I have tried to present a balanced viewpoint from both sides of the paranormal the believers and the sceptics and allow you to make up your own mind do you believe in the paranormal or not. This book will go in-depth about everything ghost hunting related, from how you can undertake your own investigation and the equipment you can use, to trying to validate your findings and even opposing viewpoints from famous believers to the most ardent sceptics. So, sit back, relax, don't turn out the light and hopefully enjoy this book.

Chapter One: What is the Paranormal?

'The spiritual life does not remove us from the world but
leads us deeper into it.'
Henri J. M. Nouwen

The paranormal according to the Oxford dictionary is
defined as: 'Something that cannot be explained by
science or reason and that seems to involve mysterious
forces.' The paranormal covers multiple subjects
including ghosts; poltergeists, Bigfoot and the Yeti,
unexplained disappearances and UFOs. The fact that the
paranormal field covers such a wide range of phenomena
it makes it much harder to investigate and distinguish
factual stories from the fictional ones. Say for example,
that there was a story of a haunting building that was
first reported in 1950. Those involved would have told
the story of that haunting to someone they knew. That
person would then go on to tell someone else what
happened but inadvertently change even the slightest of
detail and this would continue until the original story and
all the details of it are lost making it that much harder to
research and verify the actual events. To this end I am
not trying to say everything you will read in this book
will be true, rather that I will take the viewpoint of that
of a paranormal investigator and a parapsychologist.
That of a believer and a sceptic, only adding my opinion
where necessary and leave the final decision in the most
important hands, that of you, the reader.

Some people believe that ghost hunters and a paranormal investigator are one and the same, in most aspects they are but in others in my opinion they are not. Ghost hunters will go to a reportedly haunted location to see if they can capture evidence of the paranormal in order to prove that ghosts exist. A paranormal investigator on the other hand will investigate the history of a location in detail, speak with eyewitnesses who claim to have seen paranormal activity and try to validate these before deciding whether to conduct an investigation. A ghost hunting team will most likely be quite small and consist of like-minded individuals trying to capture evidence such as ghost photography, EVPs and unexplained activity such as moving objects. A paranormal investigation team works in a similar fashion, but the team may also consist of mediums and parapsychologist or sceptic so that any evidence can be reviewed to see if there is a natural explanation to any recorded phenomena. This is not to say that one way of investigating is right and the other is wrong it's just to show there are different ways to investigating the paranormal. Think of it like this if you will, the ghost hunters are the heart of the paranormal and the paranormal investigators are its head.

If we are to believe that ghosts are real, we must consider that there is more than one type. The most common type of ghost is called an interactive spirit. Interactive spirits are believed to be that of deceased loved ones. These spirits are said to make themselves known most commonly from odours, for example, a particular type of perfume that one would associate with a person with or the more commonly reported, cigarette smoke. The next type of ghost is known as a residual haunting. A residual haunting is said to be like echoes of the past reaching out to the present day and repeating the events that took place when the ghost passed away. One of the most famously reported residual haunting is that of the Ninth Legion of Rome. Documented sightings have reported spotting the legion passing the Treasure House in York marching down the old Roman road which is eighteen inches below the ground and would explain why they are allegedly only seen from the knees up. Residual haunting is also known as stone tape theory. This theory is that ghosts and reported hauntings work much like that of EVP recordings and that during traumatic events they can be projected in the form of energy which can be imprinted onto items such as rocks and then under certain conditions they can be replayed. Could this type of trauma explain while the Legion still marches to this day? We may never know.

The next type of ghost can be more frightening and traumatic of all those involved; this spirit is known as a poltergeist. Poltergeist consists of two German words 'poltern' meaning noisy and 'geist' meaning ghost. The typical phenomena associated with this type of spirit typically can consist of inanimate objects being thrown regardless of size, banging electrical disturbances and in extreme cases physical attacks on those who witness the activity.

Finally, there is the most disturbing but rare ghost known as demonic or negative entities. Demonic entities are believed to consist of pure negative energy. In Christian demonology, a demon is said to be an unclean spirit that can cause demonic possessions. These entities are often witnessed as large black masses with no shape or form. I must warn all those who read this while I have never personally encountered a demonic entity, it is unwise to provoke them as it is believed that they can inflict both physical and psychological harm. It is believed that the most common form of a demonic or negative attack is that of three scratch marks that cannot be explained naturally as this is believed to be a mocking of the holy trinity.

Chapter Two: Old School Equipment

'The paranormal, you can't pick and choose it's all or
nothing.'
Zak Bagans

You have seen them, right? These ghost hunting TV
shows using all modern-day technology to locate and
validate paranormal activity? It wasn't always this way,
and the average ghost hunter doesn't have the large-scale
budget that these shows have. This is why sometimes we
rely on what I call old school equipment. These items of
equipment, in my opinion can often be more reliable
than new technology because they have been used for
hundreds of years by paranormal investigators.

Compass

The compass is the original EMF detector. Ghosts are
believed to be made up of electromagnetic energy so if
there is a change to the Electromagnetic field, in theory a
fluctuation of energy will cause the compass point move.
For the most accurate results, the compass should be
placed on an even surface to prevent the investigator
from accidently interfering with the compass and in turn
giving a false reading.

Pen and paper

'The pen is mightier than the sword' as the saying goes. These simple tools are some of the most important items of equipment that an investigator can have. The simple reason for this is because it is important to document the dates and times of any paranormal activity that you potentially encounter. This includes base EMF and temperature readings so that fluctuations can be recorded for comparison for future investigations or to see if there is a logical explanation for the activity. A pen and paper are also useful to document trigger objects and if there is any movement. To do this place a piece of paper on a flat surface and draw around the trigger object for example a cross take a picture and leave the room sealed for an agreed upon time. When you return see if there has been any movement and if you are unsure check the photograph you took for comparison. These tools are also used to document eyewitness reports in regard to paranormal activity but for also documenting any findings and names given by a medium if you are working with one, so that you can research any information received to verify after the investigation. These tools were often used by mediums in the spiritualist movement as a form of divination to receive messages from spirits, it's known as automatic or spirit writing. (See Divination Techniques)

Flour dusting

The practice of flour dusting has been used by investigators to validate paranormal activity for many years. The investigator would choose an area that has reports of moving objects and surround the area with a sprinkling of flour. The area should then be sealed off so that outside influences can't affect the experiment. If the object has moved there should be clear impressions in the flour showing how much the object has moved or even a handprint.

Torch

Trust me, this item is a must have. Most of the locations you will investigate (which will mostly be at night) are often badly lit but at least with a good torch you will always find your way.

First Aid Kit

As mentioned above, some of the places you will investigate will be run down and in a bad state of repair. This means you are more likely to suffer from; slips, trips, cuts and falls so access to a first aid kit is essential in case you have to deal with these situations.

String

Sometimes the simplest of items can be the most effective tools to investigate claims of paranormal activity. A piece of string can be placed on door handles and secured to the frame on doors that are reported to slam on their own. This experiment should be filmed by a locked of camera so if the string is broken you can view the footage to see if a logical explanation can be found. An example of this investigation technique can be seen in Peter Underwood's 'The Ghost Hunters guide: Illustrated Edition. In the book he explains that while he was investigating an alleged haunted house that he suspected that the tenets young daughter could be responsible for the activity. To test his theory, once the girl had gone to bed, he placed the string on the door so that if she left the room the string would be broken. Later into the investigation it is revealed that a plant pot had moved so Underwood checked the string on the daughter's door, it had been broken.

Pendulums

Most commonly referred to as a crystal pendulum. Crystals are allegedly able to store energy which the spirits can then use to manipulate causing the pendulum to move. An investigator will generally ask yes or no questions and ask the spirits to move the pendulum in the corresponding direction, for example, forwards and backwards for yes and side to side for no. The most effective way to use a pendulum is to leave it on a stand situated on a flat and level surface so that subconscious movement from someone who is holding the pendulum can be ruled out.

Ouija Board

A Ouija board is a form of divination that can be used by investigators to receive messages from the spirit world. The board is considered a form of automatic writing, a practice that dates back as far as 1100AD in China where it was called Fuji, roughly meaning planchette writing. The Ouija as we know it was created in the nineteenth century when businessman Elijah Bond patented the board and planchette that has become the iconic product that we know today. The board consists of YES and NO, 0-9, A-Z and GOODBYE and it is believed that spirits can use the combined energy of those using it, to move the planchette. Many religious figures have called the boards a tool of the devil and the occult and using such tools could lead to demonic possession. Many involved in the scientific community dispute the paranormal powers of the Ouija board as they believe a more logical explanation is that it relies on the ideomotor effect to move the planchette and we are not actually contacting spirits but our own deep subconscious. While I remain sceptical of the supernatural powers of the board, I myself have an experience to which I could not find a logical explanation. During my time working with a psychic, I was conducting an Ouija board session with four strangers who were waiting for a reading. I was not using the board personally and only explained how to conduct the session. While these individuals were using the board, information was being received that was relevant and personal to me and to this day I still wonder how this was possible. To those who are set on using a board I will offer some advice. First, never under any circumstances use a board on your own. I say this because while you are on your own you are more susceptible to the alleged phenomena associated with Ouija boards you may cause yourself harm because you can scare yourself into believing any messages you receive. Secondly, never use one in a graveyard; this is just disrespectful to all those that now reside there in peace. Thirdly, take any messages you receive with a grain of salt as you do not know if any information is relevant or if it is even a spirit you are connecting with. Lastly always close with goodbye before leaving the session, this is because some believers consider that if you do not close with goodbye, you can leave a portal open to the spirit world from which both positive and negative energies can emerge.

Did you know?

- Bonds employee William Fuld took over production and rewrote the origins of the board, claiming that the Ouija was a combination of French and German words for yes.

- The patent rights to the board were eventually sold to the Parker brothers, now Hasbro who still sell the board to this day.

- In 2001 Ouija boards were burned in New Mexico alongside books of Harry Potter by religious fundamentalist groups because they were symbols of witchcraft.

Glass Divination

Glass Divination is a technique used by some in place of an Ouija board. It requires an upturned glass, a smooth and flat surface such as a table and a group of willing participants. The participants would place a single fingertip, lightly on the glass so as not to assert too much pressure that would prevent it from moving or indeed allow someone to influence it. The glass would then be rotated clockwise to the number of people using the glass and then stop to introduce themselves to the alleged spirits.

Dowsing Rods

Dowsing rods are another form of divination usually used in attempts to locate ground water sources as well as metal ores and gemstones. Some investigators have used them in attempts to make contact with spirits in the form of copper rods. Ghosts are believed to be able to manipulate the electromagnetic field to answer questions by moving the rods or even to locate the spirits. The scientific and sceptic community believe the rods rely on the ideomotor effect much like that of pendulums.

Glass of water

You may think that there wouldn't be much use for a glass of water in a paranormal investigation however this is far from the truth, because for many years paranormal investigators such as Harry Price have used this method to effectively debunk possible paranormal activity. Placing a glass of water where objects have reportedly moved on their own will show if the activity is down to nothing more than natural vibrations which are causing objects to move on their own.

Thermometer

The thermometer is used to give investigators temperature readings of their surroundings. There have been numerous reports throughout the years that ghosts are able to affect the temperature in an attempt to make their presence known through phenomena known as cold spots.

Camera

Cameras have been used in an attempt to document proof of the afterlife since its invention; this technique is known as spirit photography. Throughout history there have been many hoaxes produced, however there has also been evidence captured that keep sceptics pondering as to their authenticity to this day. One of the most famous spirit photographs captured is that of the Brown Lady of Raynham Hall. When taking photographs be aware of the atmosphere around you. What I mean by this is if you are investigating a location and the conditions are cold your breath will be visible and when taking a photograph you could mistake this for a 'ghostly mist.' Also be careful with the camera flash and dust particles and bugs as when taking a photograph these could be mistaken for orbs and other anomalies.

Tape EVP recorder

These are much like today's digital recorders however, these older recorders made use of tape that had to be rewound in order to play back. The trouble with the tape recorders is that often people would just re-record over old tape, and this could potentially leave false recordings as not all of the information the tape would be deleted.

Chapter Three: Modern Equipment

'Nine times out of ten we find reasons for everything
going on that isn't paranormal.'
Brian Robertson

As the field of paranormal research advances, so does
that of the equipment used to try and validate the
existence of ghosts. Some of these items are widely used
now in the industry but we must always remember that
they aren't without their flaws.

Accelerometer

An accelerometer is a device which is used to detect
forces such as movement or vibrations that are presented
in a wavelength graph. The device is useful for
debunking reports of paranormal activity as it can help
locate the source, for example the slightest of vibrations
may cause items to move naturally.

EMF detectors

EMF detectors are one of the most commonly used
pieces of equipment used in paranormal investigations. It
is said that ghosts are able to manipulate the
electromagnetic field which these devices are able to
detect. These devices come in many different forms, the
most common being a small handheld detector that
consists of five LEDs, the higher the light displays the

higher the energy reading. EMF detectors are not infallible however as they can pick up the background electromagnetic energy from live or recently used power cables to other pieces of equipment, so before conducting a full investigation it is wise to first get base readings of EMF of a location to rule these out as possible sources for the phenomena.

EMF Pump

An EMF Pump is believed to generate EMF which the spirits can then use in order to produce evidence of paranormal activity such as clearer EVP recordings or using the additional energy in order to manifest on a camera or photograph.

EVP Recorders

In the world of the paranormal electronic voice phenomena are sounds that are recorded in devices that can be interpreted as spirit voices or sounds that weren't present on the original recording. Investigators will ask questions and will leave a set amount of time to allow for a possible reply before moving onto the next one. EVPs are generally put into three categories depending on the quality of the recording, these are:

- Class A: The EVP is clear, and it is easy to understand what is being said.

- Class B: Is usually less distinct that a class A and may require several replays to comprehend what is being said.

- Class C: This class of EVP will often require the use of computer software to discern what is being said.

The EVPs you capture should be played back live to avoid the possibility of fraudulent or contaminated evidence. When recording questions, it is best to stand still and be as quiet as possible to rule out any potential false evidence. My advice would be that if you manage to capture any potential activity on the recorder is to leave the guessing game until you get the opportunity to analyse the evidence in more detail. The reason I suggest this is because it will rule out confirmation bias and pareidolia, this is where because one person hears something when it is played back a second time our brain will use this suggestion to recognise the unexplained phenomena.

Mel Meter

A Mel Meter is a handheld device that has a display that shows real time EMF and temperature readings. The device comes with a built-in alarm that alerts the user should there be a sudden change in either of the fields.

Motion Sensors & Motion activated cameras

Investigators use motion sensors as trigger objects to try and trace spirits movements at a location. The sensors are placed in areas where apparitions have been reported and if they are triggered, they produce an alert to let the investigators check for activity. The motion activated cameras are usually used in wildlife photography however some paranormal investigators have used them to try and capture paranormal activity. These devices are susceptible to outside influences as some sensors detect even the smallest of vibrations from objects such as passing cars, falling debris or even wild animals can cause them to go off. The most effective way to debunk outside influences is to record the devices with a locked off camera to show if anything has set them off accidently.

Laser pen

Some investigators use laser pens in attempts to capture paranormal activity. The laser pen can be used in doorways to see if a spirit can break the line, or the pen can be set out as a grid to see if a spirit outline can be mapped by the dots becoming blacked out.

SLS Camera

The SLS camera is a recent advancement in the paranormal equipment field. The camera makes use of the Xbox Kinect system to map out any movement in the shape of stick figures. Investigators will often combine the SLS with trigger objects to see if a figure can be mapped out touching the item. While the technology seems to be effective, some sceptics believe that the anomalies that are detected could just be a form of software glitch while others believe we do not have enough data to make anything more than a guess.

Spirit Box

When I was a paranormal investigator, this was one of my favourite pieces of equipment. A spirit box is an audio device that rapidly scans through AM and FM frequencies to create a white noise static and allow ghost to converse with the user by selecting words. While this method can be quite successful and produce some good results, sceptics have argued that the word selection is produced by that of chance when the scan stops longer on one frequency than others as it sweeps them and thus you are just picking up the words from radio broadcasts that are happening when conducting the session. It is also completely possible that the device can suffer from confirmation bias if the session is being conducted by several people.

Ovilus

The Ovilus is a device that is said to capture energy or electromagnetic waves and then convert it into words.

While this piece of equipment can be quite impressive and sometimes produces results, sceptics are of the opinion that it is simply a random word generator and not a valid form of research.

Paranormal Apps

The rise in popularity of paranormal shows such as Ghost Adventures and Ghost Hunters who use high tech tools to search for ghosts has also caused an increase of alleged 'ghost hunting apps' that people can download in order to conduct their own ghost hunts. I would be hesitant to rely too heavily on these as they are not proven to be effective to catch actual paranormal activity. An example in my opinion would be an app called 'Paratek', while some ghost hunters and reviews of the app say they have received relevant responses I never have personally. Remember after all, the app is marketed as an 'AI speech generator.' To test its accuracy, I once turned the scan speed up to maximum and found that I generally received at least one word every two to five seconds, so my house is either extremely crowded by some very chatty ghosts or logically, it is nothing more than it is marketed, a random word generator.

Thermal Imaging devices

These devices the user temperature reading of the immediate area but is also can be used as a camera to capture temperature anomalies known as cold spots, which is believed to be that of a ghostly presence.

Your Mind

I wanted to mention this because your mind is the most powerful tool you have, especially when investigating the paranormal. One must always have an open mind and use rational thought to find and rule out any natural explanation for activity before claiming it to be paranormal. For example, if you hear a banging noise try asking questions, was it spirit? Or could it possibly be old radiators banging, floorboards creaking or falling debris which are causing the phenomena.

Chapter Four: Equipment Experiments

'To be the best, you have to have the right equipment at
your disposal.'
Hafthor Bjornsson

Now you've seen some of the equipment that paranormal
investigators have used throughout history in order to
capture evidence of activity, it's time to try out some
experiments that may help you do the same. Keep in
mind that you could investigate a location for hours and
never capture any activity. Some of these experiments
you may have seen used on paranormal investigation
shows and others I have created to show you the
different ways which you can combine your equipment
to try and corroborate your findings.

Era Cues and Trigger Objects

An era cue is a term used to describe a where a
paranormal investigator tries to replicate past situations
associated with a location in order to encourage spiritual
activity. Trigger objects are items that are either
associated with a haunting or may cause activity for
example a child spirit may interact with a teddy bear.
Below are a list of locations and era cues and trigger
objects that may be useful in trying to find paranormal
activity.

Abandoned Churches

Era cues that would be useful at this location include bell ringing, reciting the Bible, prayers, hymns, psalms and playing organ music. The trigger objects that might be useful at this location include holy water, bible, crucifix, prayer beads, thirty pieces of silver and a pentagram.

Places of Battle

Era cues that would be useful at these locations include air raid sirens; sounds of bombs dropping, marching sounds, gunfire and asking for name, rank and number. Trigger objects for this location could include dog tags; bullet casings, war medals and pictures and articles related to war.

Theatres

Era cues that would be useful at this location include shouting Macbeth on the stage as the superstition is that in saying the name of the play or quoting lines from it, will unleash bad luck to those involved. Reciting lines from plays and creating applause. The trigger objects that might be useful at this location include Cues cards, using stage props, old theatre programs and wearing costumes.

Hospitals

While rare there are some former hospitals such as Saint Catherine's Hospital in Doncaster which are open to paranormal investigation teams. Era cues that might produce evidence at these locations are calling out for help, playing a heart rate monitor sound that eventually flat lines and ambulance sirens. Trigger objects to use at this location include stethoscope; first aid kit, thermometers and wearing clothing associated with the location.

Schools

There are still some former school sites that still exist such as Ragged School Museum in London that allow paranormal investigations. Examples of era cues to use at these locations include bell ringing; whistle blowing and children's laughter. Trigger objects that may be useful include a cane, blackboard and chalk, a bell and workbooks.

Accelerometer Experiment

In the early days of paranormal investigations and in the spiritualist movement there was a belief that ghosts communicated through noises such as knocks and rapping, indeed it is a belief some still hold today. All you will need for this experiment is a flat surface and an accelerometer which can be downloaded onto a handheld device. Place the device on a flat surface and start up the App, ask the spirit to communicate through knocking or by copying your knocking. On the graph you should see the vibrations that you caused by knocking and if there is a knock heard after yours the result should be shown on the graph. While conducting this experiment be sure to rule out outside interference with the app such as team members moving, or movement caused by passing vehicles such as cars and trains.

Dowsing Rods

Here is an interesting experiment you can conduct using dowsing rods that can help eliminate the ideomotor effect, all you will need are the rods, a wooden block with a hole drilled at each end and yes and no cards. First place the rods on a flat and even surface and place the handles of the rods into each hole so they are secure, but the rods still have free movement. Finally place the yes and no cards under a corresponding rod and ask basic yes or no questions to see if the spirits can manipulate the rods to answer the question.

EMF and Compass

All you will need is two EMF meters, two compasses and two pieces of card with yes and no written on them. Place the EMF meters on a flat surface apart from each other and then place a compass close to each meter so that it isn't giving off false readings then place a yes card above one meter and the no card above the other. Finally begin asking yes or no questions to see if the spirits can manipulate the electromagnetic field to set off the EMF meter. If in theory, the EMF meter does go off, the compass should also show movement towards where the magnetic energy is strongest.

Flour and Trigger Object

This is one of the oldest investigation techniques used to try and capture paranormal activity. All you will need is a trigger object a locked off camera and a room that can be locked off so there is no chance of evidence contamination. Place a light dusting of flour on the surface and place the trigger object over the top of the area. Point the locked off camera at the trigger object making sure that its close enough that it will capture movement but also that the shot is wide enough to see around so you can debunk interference with the experiment then lock the area off for a set amount of time (usually around half an hour to an hour) Once the time has passed, return to the room and document any signs of movement if there have been any or any displacement of flour and then review the footage to see if anything has been captured.

Motion Detection Camera

There are two potential experiments you can conduct using this camera. The first experiment is to leave the camera in an area that is reported to have a large amount of reported activity and seal the area off, so no one accidently sets the equipment off. Return after a set amount of time to see if the camera has caught any activity. The other experiment is following the same steps in suggestion one but placing a trigger object in the cameras field of view. If something tries to interact with the object the camera in theory, should capture the activity.

Sensory Deprivation Ouija Board

As strange as this experiment might sound, it is definitely one that will test the credibility of the Ouija Board. First of all you will need an Ouija Board, two investigators who will be blindfolded and be using noise reduction equipment so they cannot see or hear what is happening and two investigators, one to ask questions and one to tap each Ouija user on the shoulder to let them know when a question has been asked. When all participants are ready begin by asking a question such as ''Can you tell me spirit, are you male or female'' and when you have asked it to tap the investigators on the shoulder. Watch for planchette movement and take down any letters or numbers that it may point to. Once you

34

believe the experiment has been conducted long enough tap the team members twice on the shoulder to let the users know the experiment has ended. I wonder if you will receive anything relevant or if like the sceptics claim it relies on our own subconscious suggestions. If you want to make the experiment even more interesting, if you have enough team members you could always conduct an uncontrolled Ouija Board session at the same time as this so you can compare the results.

SLS and Trigger Object

First find a flat surface where you can place the trigger object, once you have done this place a piece of paper under the trigger object and trace around it with a pen. The reason for this is that it will make it easier to determine if the item has moved. Next set up your Kinect SLS system and once its booted begin asking questions and enquire if any spirits can interact with the trigger object that you've set up. If you do manage to capture a 'stick figure' appearing to interact with the object, be sure when you have concluded the experiment to check your tracing and see if the object has moved and if so, by how much.

Chapter Five: Conducting an Investigation

'I just don't want to believe; I want to know.'
Anon

The Team

There are many different ways you could structure a team for an investigation and while each team will be different here, I will give a recommendation based on my own experiences. Try to keep the number of investigators a minimum, possibly a maximum of six. The reason I say this is while you can cover more ground in a large team at the same time the more people at a location, the higher the chance of contamination of evidence or false evidence being collected. First off you will need a lead paranormal investigator. The lead investigator will be the focus point of the investigation, usually by leading the questioning when conducting such techniques as EVP sessions. Depending on your viewpoint you may consider having a medium on the team. Mediums are believed to be able to contact the spirits of a haunted location and thus provide information that may prove useful for your investigation. On the other side of paranormal, you may wish to work with a qualified parapsychologist or sceptics, whose purpose will be to focus on finding logical explanations that may be the real cause of activity. I would also recommend working with both a technical expert and a researcher. These team members are the backbone of the investigation because without them reviewing the evidence that is captured, it is that much harder to validate and prove that any information received either via the medium or from the evidence collected from the investigation is relevant and true.

Documenting and Researching

Before heading to a location, it is important to conduct as much research as possible about the history of it, as any evidence you may find can then later be validated by facts. While on location, before conducting the main investigation, you should conduct base line tests. Base line tests are where you document the temperature and EMF of each area you intend to investigate so that there is a fluctuation you can document how much of a change there is. Conducting these tests will also allow you to rule out natural background readings such as those given off from working power lines which would affect the EMF levels and be a rational explanation for the fluctuations. In regard to the temperature, allow a few degrees in change depending on the amount of people investigating the area as there would be a natural temperature rise. While on location, you may also want to take a look around the area to see if they are anything that could be affecting the location, for example are train tracks close to locations? If so what time, do they pass in the time frame of activity of moving objects so could it be the vibrations from a passing train are the reason for activity rather than paranormal. Another thing to check would be if a location is close to power lines or power plants. If there are power lines running close by this could explain high EMF readings but also there is research that living close to these particular areas can be affected both physically and mentally by them and thus could be considered a factor in reported activity. If you work with a medium, you should record all information that they provide so you can try to validate it once the investigation is concluded. Finally, never forget the three most important pieces of information you will need. Time, date and location as the more thorough you are, the more concrete your information will be when you present it.

Example of questions for eyewitnesses:

- Do you believe in ghosts?
- Did you investigate to see if there was a natural explanation for the paranormal phenomena?
- What paranormal activity did you witness?
- Do you have any physical evidence to corroborate your experience?
- Were you alone during your experience?
- How much did you know about the history of the location before your experience?

If you are looking for good examples of how to set out investigation paperwork, be sure to check out these books.

- Paperwork and Templates for the Ghost Hunter by
  Peter Dernhill
- Ghost-Hunting for dummies by Zak Bagans
- The Ghost Hunters Guide Illustrated Edition by Peter
  Underwood

The Equipment

As you would have seen from the previous chapters, there is a wide range of equipment available to choose from. If you are conducting your first investigation, I would recommend focusing more on some of the old school equipment such as torches, a compass and a thermometer and only a few modern items such as an EVP recorder and a digital camera. The reason for this is because you may have observed someone conducting an investigation and thought to yourself 'I could do that' however when conducting an investigation yourself, a lot of patience and time is required and you may find that in fact, it is not for you and you don't enjoy it so at least the cost you have put into finding out will be minimal.

The Investigation

As mentioned in the documenting part of the investigation process your first task at a location should be to take base reading of the temperature and EMF in the areas you will be investigating so document changes to either that may be recorded later. My next piece of advice would be to introduce yourself and announce your intentions. This step may seem strange but if there is truly an afterlife and ghosts, it doesn't hurt to be polite. Because you will be working in a team, decide what equipment they will be using and who will be working with whom. This is because you may wish to run two simultaneous investigations at the same time in different areas so you can cover more of the location in less time. This could also be an experiment to see if one team can record more activity than the other. In regard to how long you spend using each piece of equipment depends on how long you intend to investigate. In a short hour-long investigation, I would say spend ten minutes using each piece of equipment, however if you are conducting a longer vigil then I would recommend twenty minutes (ten minutes to investigate and 10 minutes to review the potential evidence). When conducting an EVP session, I have always found it easier to have set questions ready to ask this is in part because you are less likely to stumble on your words and the audio should be clearer. Try to stand completely still and as quiet as possible to reduce the chance of producing false activity such as the sound of your own or the team's footsteps. Finally remember no matter how long you spend at a location you may never capture any evidence of the paranormal, remember I did say to keep an open mind not everywhere is going to be haunted.

Examples of EVP questions:

- What is your name please spirit?
- How did you die/when did you die?
- Why do you remain here?
- Would you like us to leave?
- How many spirits reside here?

Evidence Review

You've spent what seems like endless hours conducting the investigation, perhaps you are looking forward to a rest? Unfortunately, investigations don't just end when you leave a location. Depending on how long the investigation was you will have potentially hours of audio, photography and film to review, it's time to divide and conquer. Assigning team members to focus on different evidence reviews will reduce the overall workload and make it less time consuming and stressful to go through. Always keep original copies of all the files you have so if you have to enhance anything such as photographs or audio you have something to compare them to. With audio recordings, keep a log sheet to note times of possible phenomena so once you have finished you can go back to those points to examine them in greater detail by using audio analysing software. In regard to video and photographic evidence, document times of possible activity and use video editing software to enhance the quality and verify or debunk any activity you may have captured. Remember that sometimes what may seem to be a figure or orbs may actually be cause by problems with the cameras software or even reflected surfaces shining back light to the camera causing the illusion of an orb.

Final Advice

- Never investigate alone there is safety in numbers and should you injure yourself at least there is someone on hand to help.

- Be sure you conduct a risk assessment for each site that you investigate as the health and safety of you and your crew is paramount.

- If investigating on private property make sure to have the land-owner's permission to be there preferably in writing as sometimes someone may report you to the police if they see you, not knowing you have permission to be there.

- Be respectful, if there is such a thing as ghosts, would you want to be taunted or commanded to do something? Manners shouldn't end because they are ghosts.

- Make sure all equipment is fully charged and you have spare batteries or charging equipment in case of sudden power drainage.

- Avoid smoking or wearing strong smelling cologne as the smells may be picked up by others and mistaken for paranormal odours or even prevent you from picking up on genuine ones.

Chapter Six: Investigation Ideas

'No man can hope to find out the truth without
investigation.'
George F. Richards

Not every investigation you conduct will be the same.
You could go to one of the reportedly most haunted
locations in the world, capture nothing yet visit a
location that doesn't have as much exposure to the
paranormal and capture no end of evidence. This chapter
is dedicated to different approaches to investigating to
see if changing your mindset can change your outlook on
the paranormal.

Two-pronged approach investigation

For this first experiment, all you need is a location with
reported activity and enough members of your team that
you can split into two different groups. Team one will
focus on the use of older equipment to try and capture
activity and team two will focus on using the using
technology to do the same. You do not have to use the
items I have listed here; it is just to give you an example
of what equipment you could use for this experiment.
While on location each area will be investigated by each
team separately but for the same amount of time. The
aim of this experiment is to see if one style of

investigating can affect the amount of evidence you could capture.

Team One (Old Tech)

- Polaroid camera or any old type of camera
- Dictaphone
- Compass
- String (use like a laser grid if the line is broken investigate)
- Dowsing Rods
- Crystal Pendulums
- Ouija Board
- Balls and chalk to mark trigger objects

Team Two (New Tech)

- Digital Camera
- EVP digital recorder
- EMF meter
- Laser Grid
- Digital thermometer
- Spirit Box

Battle of the Sexes investigation

Here is a question; can your gender make you more open to the suggestion of the paranormal? It is a question I'm sure that will spark a debate between friends and family but there is a reason I pose this philosophical question. A study conducted in 2009 found that women are twice as likely to visit a fortune-teller or psychic as men. Without wishing to stereotype, if you were to pick up a magazine dedicated to the subject of spirits and mediumship you will notice that the vast majority of advertisements are for female mediums; however, this is not the case when it comes to the world of paranormal investigations, where you will find the majority of investigators are male, why is this? Could it be that men take a more practical approach to the paranormal by not using their intuition, but finding the right tool for the job whereas a woman would be more likely try to connect emotionally to a location? To test this idea here is what I propose, you will have two teams, team one will be the ladies and team two will be the men. Both teams will investigate the same location for the same amount of time and use the same equipment as each other. Once the investigations have concluded, it's time to examine the team's evidence, I wonder which team will capture the most evidence?

Ley Lines Investigation

Ley Lines are believed to be geographical straight lines of power crossing all over the world that run through historical landmarks such as Stonehenge. While the scientific community and archaeologists regard ley lines as a pseudoscience and pseudo archaeology some in the paranormal community believe that the natural earth energies that run along the ley lines can contribute to increased paranormal activity. So, could this be true? Well, the aim of this investigation would be to try and see if there is any evidence to support this viewpoint. Firstly, you will need to study ley lines near your location and look for reportedly haunted locations on or close to the line that you could investigate. You should aim to investigate several locations and look to conclude your investigation where the ley lines cross or meet up to see if there is more paranormal activity the closer you are to the connecting ley lines.

Different Paranormal Backgrounds Investigation

As you know there are many different approaches to the paranormal. You have mediums, who believe they have the ability to communicate with the spirits world naturally through their gifts. You have paranormal investigators who seek to provide definitive proof that there is an afterlife using equipment to gather evidence and finally you have the sceptics who do not believe there is such a thing as paranormal. The aim of this investigation is to bring all of these viewpoints together to see how each group's experiences will differ but also to see if any corroborating evidence of the paranormal can be found. The investigation will take place at a single location over several days. The first investigation will focus on the mediums using their gifts to pick up as much information as possible. One member from the paranormal team should be with them in order to take notes on all the information they receive. The second investigation will focus on the paranormal investigators using their equipment to see if they can gather any paranormal evidence or validate any information that the psychics pick up in the previous day's investigation. Day threes investigation will be the sceptics, seeing if they can find any logical explanations for the reported paranormal activity or the evidence collected by the teams. The final experiment will mix all of the teams together; the reason for this is because it will be interesting to see how having the different backgrounds together will affect not only the activity but the teams' findings.

Chapter Seven: Psychic Abilities and Divination Techniques

'Divination is a means of telling ourselves what we already know.'
Joanne Harris

The word psychic derives from the Greek word 'psychikos' meaning 'of the mind.' You might be surprised to hear that the term psychic is actually broader than you think, as there are many different abilities associated with it. Here are some of the abilities that are associated with psychics.

Clairvoyance

Clairvoyance is the term used to generally describe a psychic; however it was originally used to describe someone who would receive psychic messages in the form of pictures.

Clairaudience

Clairaudience is the term used to describe when a psychic can hear a message from the spirit world.

Clairsentience

Clairsentience is the ability to feel psychic information and is often used to describe where a medium receives information that wasn't clairvoyant or clairaudient. Those who claim to use this ability tend to focus on psychic healing work such as reiki and crystal healing.

Clairtangency

Clairtangency is the ability to receive psychic information or impressions through touching. Many believe that a person can imprint emotions and memories onto items (stone tape theory) which can then be read by those who utilise this ability. This ability is often referred to as Psychometry which we will discuss further on in this chapter.

Clairgustance

Clairgustance is the ability to taste something without consuming anything that causes the sensation.

Clairalience

Clairalience is the ability to pick up on psychic smells without their being a rational explanation for what is causing it. The smells could be connected or associated with an individual or situation. Most dismiss this ability as there are usually logical explanations for what is causing the smell.

Precognition

Precognition comes from the Latin words 'prae' meaning before and 'cognitio' meaning acquiring knowledge. Precognition is the ability to become aware of future events. One of the earliest studies into this phenomenon was the Greek philosopher Aristotle. He believed that while some dreams may be the cause of future events, they were nothing more than mere coincidence. There have been many of these 'coincidences' experienced by people throughout history, one of whom was President Lincoln. Lincoln is said to have foreseen his own death, not long before his death he was awakened by the sound of sobbing, upon entering the east wing of the White House he saw a corpse whose face was covered. 'Who is dead?' he asked the mourners, 'The president' was the reply 'he was killed by an assassin' Lincoln would be assassinated by John Wilkes Booth. Perhaps one of the most famous examples of precognition was a man called Nostradamus. Nostradamus was a French seer who wrote the book Les Prophéties, a collection of quatrains that allegedly predicted future events. Some of these events that Nostradamus allegedly predicted were The Great Fire of London, The French Revolution, both World Wars and Adolf Hitler's rise to power. Sceptics and scholars have rebutted these claims saying that the so-called prophecies are so vague that they are open to interpretation and this is why most of them are able to fit into situations that have already happened. Another famous example would be that of author Morgan Robertson. In1898 Robertson wrote 'The wreck of the Titan' a story of a British passenger ship liner called the SS Titan. The events of the book are eerily similar to that of the RMS Titanic that sank after hitting an iceberg in 1912. This has led many to believe that Robertson foresaw the events of the Titanic and used it as the basis for his book. So, what do you believe? Was it coincidence or was it a case of precognition?

Psychokinesis

Psychokinesis is the ability to manipulate objects with the powers of our minds. One of the most famous practitioners of this alleged ability is Uri Geller who is known for his ability to bend spoons. His claims however have been challenged by magicians such as James Randi who showed that magicians had been using this 'ability' to fool their audiences for years and that it requires nothing more than sleight of hand and some preparation time. Scientists have long since dismissed that Psychokinesis is possible as it violates may established laws of physics such as the second law of thermodynamics which to summarise states that as energy is transferred or transformed, more and more of it is wasted.

Out of Body Experiences

An out of body experience is the name attributed to the phenomenon where a person feels their consciousness has left their body. Experiences of an out of body experience include an awareness that your body is distant or below you, the ability to view yourself or a scene from an impossible angle and the ability to move through walls and other objects. Scientists believe that this phenomenon take place inside a person's mind and are just simply some kind of hallucination. They also believe that those who claim to have experienced these situations, often have had their brains starved of oxygen for a time. Scientists have also shown drug such as ketamine can produce similar effects to those of out of body experiences.

Remote Viewing

Remote viewing is the ability to solely use the mind in order to give details of a place, object or person without physically having interacted with them. During the Cold War era both the Soviet Union and the United States were taking a keen interest in psychic phenomenon. It was during this time the United States' CIA started conducted experiments to conclude weather the phenomenon could have use within the military; it was codenamed 'Stargate Project.'

Testing For Extra Sensory Perception

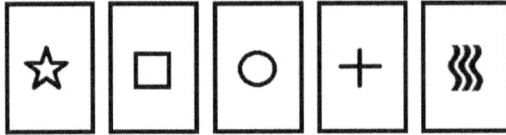

Zener Cards

Zener Cards are a pack of twenty-five cards, each with five different symbols as shown above. The cards were created by Karl Zener and J.B Rhine in order to test claims of alleged ESP abilities. Much of their work was discredited at the time due to the lack of control measures in place, for example the original cards were found to be too translucent and the symbols could be seen through the card. Once control measures were implicated correctly there was a huge decline in results to the point that they average correct answers which are between 3-7 are nothing more than a product of chance, Zener cards are now no longer used to test psychic abilities. I would recommend giving it a try, all you need is a blank pack of twenty-five cards and a marker pen and to draw the above symbols five times each. Next shuffle the cards and place them face down on a level surface, close your eyes and concentrate on the cards, picture the image of the top card in your mind and once you see it clearly state the symbol out loud before turning the card over. So how well did you do?

The Ganzfeld Experiment

This is the experiment used to test for telepathy. The test is a form of sensory deprivation, the recipient known as a receiver, is played white noise through headphones and their eyes are covered with half ping pong balls that then have a red light shone through them. The sensory deprivation lasts less than an hour and during this time a 'sender' will try to pass information on to the receiver. During this time, the receiver will describe what sense and see which is then recorded by the controller of the experiment. The experiment has been heavily criticised by critics such as Professor Richard Wiseman who claim that not all the experiments that have been carried out took place with correct control conditions such as sound proofed rooms which could lead to sensory leakage which would influence the results. To this date there has been no consistency in the results from the tests.

Divination comes from the Latin word 'divinare' which means 'to foresee'. Throughout the years there have been many forms of divination from Uromancy (divination by observing urine) to Tyromancy (Divination by writing questions on cheese to determine answers) I kid you not. If you are interested in finding out more of these bizarre techniques, be sure to check out 'The Element Encyclopaedia of The Psychic World' to discover more, here though we will focus more on the classic techniques you may come across.

Tarot Cards

Tarot cards are a deck of seventy-eight cards consisting of twenty-two Major arcana and fifty-six minor cards. The deck has of four sets which are commonly referred to as Swords, Cups, Pentacles and Wands and much like a standard deck of cards consist of numbered cards Ace to King. Tarot cards can be used in a number of ways but most readers use them to give insight into someone's personal life. A basic three card reading will represent a person's past, present and future an example of which I have provided below.

- Past: The Tower

A disaster that has hurt you in the past such as a health issue has knocked yourself-esteem and you need to rebuild from this.

- The Present: Ace of Wands

There is a new beginning on the horizon for you because you have started a new lifestyle chance this could be a new diet of fitness regime; this will boost your self confidence that you have been lacking.

- The future: Nine of Cups

The nine of cups stands for abundance and material success, I believe that, because you have undergone such a change in fortune that you should write about your success and this will inspire others.

The issue with Tarot is you could have the same three cards in three different readings but each reader will interpret the meaning differently, for example the question you ask of the cards for example 'will my relationship last?' and then you draw the Nine of Swords. The Nine of Swords is often considered the nightmare card and because of this you may believe the relationship is doomed to fail however it could also be interpreted that as with nightmares a situation may not be as bad as it appears. Having a tarot reading whether you believe them or not is a fascinating experience and one I believe you should try it at least once, so you can truly decide for yourself.

Dowsing

See Chapter 2: Old School Equipment

Automatic Writing

Automatic writing, also known as trance or free writing is a technique used by mediums and psychotherapists as a means to gain new levels of insight and thought. During the height of the spiritualist movement mediums would utilise the technique to contact alleged spirits during séance sessions. It is believed that one of the most famous examples of automatic writing is that of The Bible, the reason being that it was written by human scribes but were acting under divine influence when doing so. Sceptics argue that much like the Ouija boards, automatic writing is a result of the ideomotor effect and that the messages we receive are not that of spirit but our own subconscious or suppressed thoughts being brought forward. To conduct an Automatic Writing exercise all you will need is a pen, paper, an alarm set with a timer and somewhere peaceful to conduct the experiment. When you are completely relaxed clear your mind of all thoughts, pick up the pen and close your eyes. Put the pen to paper and allow your hand to wander freely. After the alarm sounds open your eyes and observe what you have written, what did you write?

Psychometry

Psychometry also known as object reading, comes from the Greek words ψυχή meaning 'spirit' and μέτρον meaning 'to measure' is a technique used by mediums to obtain knowledge by only making physical contact with an inanimate object such as a ring or photograph. Mediums will pass on the information to the client without prior knowledge of the item or the person. Some sceptics believe that this technique is merely a form of hot reading and that the client is being observed for reactions to see if the statements given hold any meaning. You too can try to perform Psychometry for yourself; all you will need is a group of friends and a box with a whole big enough to fit your hand into. Without your knowledge, allow your friends to place all of their items into the box and when this is accomplished a selected member should inform you that all the items have been placed in the box. When ready place your hand into the box and pick up an item that has been placed within it. Close your eyes and concentrate, how does the object make you feel? What is it, what is the attachment to the object and who did it belong to? Express your feelings to your audience and when you believe you know what the object is and who it belongs to state this out loud. So how accurate were your Psychometry readings?

Astrology

Astrology derives its name from the Latin word astrologia meaning star study. Astrology like most forms of divination is considered a pseudoscience because it claims to be divine information about human affairs by studying the position and movement of the stars. You will most commonly see them in the form of Horoscopes in many newspapers and magazines. Sceptics have argued that horoscopes are irrelevant as they largely rely on blanket statements. A blanket statement is a sentence that is assumed to be true but applies to everything that it is being discussing. An example of a blanket statement would be 'all Librans are indecisive', or 'All Arians are hot headed.'

Palmistry

Palmistry is considered one of the oldest forms of divination with evidence of it being seen and possibly originating in China 3000BCE. In palmistry the left hand is considered to relate to a person's destiny and the right hand reveals how a person will carry out that destiny. A reader will observe the hands and reveal insights into a person's health, wellbeing, emotions, intelligence and much more.

Numerology

Numerology is the study of numbers and how they can indicate a person's aptitude and characteristics. Numerology consists of the numbers one to nine and the master numbers of eleven, twenty-two and sometimes thirty-three. There are many different ways that numerology can be used, however for the purpose of this section we will focus on western Name Numerology.

1	2	3	4	5	6	7	8	9
A	B	C	D	E	F	G	H	I
J	K	L	M	N	O	P	Q	R
S	T	U	V	W	X	Y	Z	

How it works:

As you can see from the chart above each letter is assigned a number the aim is to add up all numbers that form the basis of your name and then find the lowest number possible to find your character number, for example John Smith would be;

John: 1+6+8+5= 20 Smith: 1+4+9+8= 22

Then: 20+22= 42

And finally take 42 as the sum: 4+2= 6

So John Smiths character number would be 6

The Number's Characteristics

As with many divination techniques every individual may have a different definition for each number, for example I have taken the number references from a book titled 'Paths to predictions'

- One: Ambition, action and creative
- Two: Imagination, creative with artistic qualities
- Three: Authoritative figure, strong sense of duty
- Four: Rebellious, opposition and idealistic
- Five: excitable, always looking for the next adventure
- Six: Attractive, love of beauty and trusting

- Seven: Love of travel and a magical number linked to psychic powers
- Eight: Successful but at the expense of loneliness
- Nine: Determination, courageous but sometimes impulsive

Runes

Runes are a set of twenty-four or twenty-five small stones each bearing Norse symbols etched or drawn onto them. The term rune derives from The Germanic word root run meaning secret. Each rune comprises of vertical and diagonal lines each with their own individual meaning. Much like Tarot it is believed that runes provide the means to personal growth rather than to just provide answers. For more information on the runes meanings, be sure to check out 'The Element Encyclopaedia of Secret Signs and Symbols.'

Crystal Pendulums

See Chapter Two: Old School Equipment

Tasseomancy

Tasseomancy is a form of divination where the reader will interpret patterns that are left by loose tea leaves. It dates back to medieval Europe where on trade routes fortune tellers would use tea leaves in their divinations. While tea leaves are the most traditional method, people also perform readings by using wine sediments, coffee grinds and wax. To perform this reading using wax all you will need is a cold bowl of water and a candle. Light the candle and allow the liquid wax to build up for a few minutes. Once there is enough, blow out the candle and drip the wax into the bowl of water. The wax should solidify quite quickly and form a shape. You can find a list of meanings by performing a quick Google search.

Séances

Séance is the French word for session. A Séance is generally regarded as a gathering of individuals whose sole intent is to contact the dead the sessions are generally led by a medium. There are many different techniques used during a séance in attempts to contact the spirit world, these include Ouija boards, energy circles (where the attendees form a circle, holding hands in order to raise energy that the spirits can then allegedly use to make contact.) trance mediumship and table tipping. Table tipping is a practice when a group of individuals would sit or stand around a table, place their fingertips lightly on the table and wait to see if the table will rotate, levitate or tip in any direction. The popularity of séances saw a rise during the peak of the spiritualist movement where mediums were able to produce 'evidence' such as spirit ectoplasm, rapping in response to questions and even poltergeist activity. It was also during this time that criticisms of séances were also on the rise. Sceptics and the scientific communities consider them a scam because of a lack of inscrutable evidence, the lack of control conditions to prevent fraud and the rise in fraudulent mediums and their methods to produce paranormal activity being exposed. I would highly recommend attending a séance at least once. The experience of a séance itself is interesting and one you will never forget. In doing this you can decide for yourself if you believe it or not.

Chapter Eight: Arguments for and Against Reported Paranormal Activity

'Where there is an open mind, there will always be a frontier.'
Charles F. Kettering

Throughout history there have been reports of paranormal activity. In this chapter I will cover some of the most famous recorded cases ever documented. I will give an introduction to each then list the activity reported with each case and a section about investigations carried out at the locations. Finally, I will conclude with some doubts and sceptical opinions as to the paranormal activity's authenticity remember however, the final choice of what you believe will be down to you, do these cases warrant their reputation or are you as sceptical as ever?

The Enfield Poltergeist

The Enfield Poltergeist refers to alleged paranormal activity that took place at 284 Green Street in Enfield, London in the late 1970s. In August 1977, the police we called to residence because Peggy Hogson, the current tenant, claimed that she had witnessed furniture moving on its own and some of her children heard knocking emanating from the walls. A police constable was said to witness activity when she went to investigate but could not find a logical explanation for it. There were numerous eye-witness reports to alleged activity until it came to an end in 1979.

The activity

- Thrown objects (including heavy furniture)
- Disembodied voices
- Children levitating
- Loud bangs

The Investigation

The incident was investigated by Maurice Grosse and Guy Lyon Playfair, from the Society for Psychical Research. They documented hours of alleged paranormal activity on tape from objects being thrown, to a possible possession through one of the children, Janet. Playfair believed that a paranormal entity was to blame for the disturbances in the house but was also of the opinion that some of the activity was faked by the girls. The incident was also allegedly investigated by Ed and Larraine Warren who concluded that all events in the house had supernatural explanations.

Doubts and sceptical opinions

- Janet, one of the children was caught in trickery. A locked off hidden camera in her room caught her bending spoons.

- The two girls involved in the haunting, confessed their pranks to journalists.
- John Beloff, former president of the Society for Psychical Research, suggested that Janet was using some form of ventriloquism in order to produce the disembodied voice. This opinion was also held by Milbourne Christopher a magician and ventriloquist and ventriloquist Ray Alan.

Borley Rectory

Borley Rectory was a house that was located in Borley, Essex and once called 'The most haunted house in England' after investigations by psychic researcher Harry Price.Built in 1862 the house was the home of the Rector of Borley and his family. The house has changed hands several times until 1939 when due to a fire caused by an oil lamp it burned down. The remains of building stood in place for a time, until it was finally demolished in 1944.

The activity

- Bells ringing without explanation
- Stone and bottle throwing
- Messages through rapping sounds
- Spirit lights
- Disembodied footsteps
- Wall writing

The Harry Price Investigations

In 1937, Harry Price took out a year-long rental agreement with the owners of the property so that he would be able to conduct in-depth investigations of the Rectory. Price placed advertisements in a newspaper in May, seeking observers who would spend periods at the location with instructions to record any phenomena they witnessed. In 1938 Helen Glanville conducted a planchette session and according to Price, she contacted two spirits, one being that of a French nun called Marie Lairre, who claimed she was murdered and that she was buried in either the cellar or thrown down an old well. Price believed that the wall writings that he documented were Marie trying to communicate. One of the writings reportedly said 'Marianne, please help me get out.' Interestingly in 1943 Price conducted a brief dig of the cellar, in the ruins of the rectory and did discover two bones which after examination was believed to have belonged to a young woman.

Doubts and sceptical opinions

- Many of the legends of the Rectory were fabricated
- The children of Reverend Harry Bull claimed to have seen no activity and were surprised by the houses haunted title.
- In 1948 members of the Society for Paranormal Research wrote a book about their investigations into

Harry Prices claims and they concluded Price fraudulently produced some of the phenomena.

- The Society for Paranormal Research study 'The Borley Report' stated the phenomena reported was either due to natural causes or fictionalised evidence.
- Price was reported to be an expert conjurer, so it was possible he used these skills to fabricate evidence.
- Allegedly, one resident Marianne Foyster, the wife of Reverend Lionel Foyster was having an affair with a lodger and used the claims of paranormal activity to cover up her indiscretions.

Demon House

The Demon house is the site of reported demonic activity, including that of a possession of members of the Ammons family in Gary, Indiana in 2011. In 2012, Father Michael Maginot was granted permission by the bishop to perform an exorcism after meeting with the family and concluding that the house and its tenets were the subject of demonic activity. Father Michael reportedly conducted three exorcisms, two in English and one in Latin. The activity reportedly ceased when the Ammons family moved away from the house later that same year.

The activity

- Shadow figures
- Claims of levitation

- Physical attacks
- Possession
- Claims of choking
- Unexplained boot prints

The Investigation

In 2014, Zak Bagans purchased the house for $35,000 so he could conduct an in-depth investigation into the reported paranormal activity at the house and would document his journey and his investigation in the documentary The Demon House. In the documentary he interviewed the local police and child protective services that were called to investigate because of the extreme circumstances surrounding the activity and the family. The family themselves refused to be interviewed believing that since Zak had been in the house an entity could have attached itself to him in order to reconnect itself to the family. Dr Barry Taff who had visited the house was due to return to work with Zak more on the documentary however he was rushed to the hospital because for some unknown reason his organs as he says, 'began shutting down' and medical experts were baffled as to why this was happening. During his visit to the house a shadow figure was caught on video. Dr Taff wouldn't be the last person to be affected by the houses alleged activity. Adam, a cameraman working with Zak under-went huge psychological changes because of his time in the house, becoming erratic in his behaviour and taunting the entity that he believed had affected him. It is revealed that his whole personality changed and even he got tattoos of 666 on both his hands. A family who entered the house while filming the documentary required an exorcism on their daughter Erica, after a drastic change in her personality. At the end of his investigation Zak did a lone recorded vigil of the location where he becomes more paranoid as the investigation progresses. The investigation ended with Zak revealing that he believed he saw something emerge from the walls in the house; this allegedly caused him eye pain which would later be revealed to be diplopia (double vision). Zak demolished the house in 2016 in an attempt to end the haunting.

Doubts and sceptical opinions

- The former landlord Charles Reed stated he never experienced any activity nor did any of his previous tenants or ones that resided in the house after the family moved away
- The children were interviewed by specialists and psychologists who concluded the children engaged in deception in accordance with the mother's beliefs
- Physician Geoffrey Onyeukwu failed to witness any paranormal activity at the property and included in his medical notes stated,"delusions of ghost in home" and "hallucinations"
- Joe Nickel, a senior research fellow for the Committee for Sceptical Inquiry interviewed a number of witnesses and concluded that were

numerous explanations for the alleged paranormal events that were reported

- The house was found to have black mould in the attic. Black mould can cause dizziness, mood swings, and hallucinations and could be the logical explanation for paranormal activity that took place.

Amityville Horror

The Amityville horror story remains one of the most famous and controversial reported poltergeist hauntings of all time. The house was the site of a mass family murder committed by Ronald Joseph DeFeo Jr, who murdered his mother, father, his two brothers and his two sisters. In December 1975, it became the home of George Lutz and his family who fled the house after twenty-eight days because of the alleged paranormal activity they were experiencing.

The activity

- Strange odours
- Doors slamming
- Oozing walls
- Disembodied voices
- A priest allegedly afflicted with stigmata symptoms

Investigation by the Warrens

The Warrens were intrigued by the case and decided to investigate the house. After gathering a camera and news crew they were supposed to collect the keys from George Lutz, however according to Ed, he would only meet with them at least four blocks away from the house for fear becoming affected by the house again. When questioned by Ed about what the family experienced in the house his reply would always be the same 'You know.' Upon entering the house Ed would remark that it 'reeked of death' Ed went to investigate the cellar where he personally believes as a demonologist that evil thrives because it hates gods light. In the cellar he took out a crucifix and began to use religious provocation which he believes led to an unseen entity to physically push him to the ground. After using more provocation to free himself he returned to the rest of the crew. During the rest of the investigation they allegedly caught and apparition in a photograph that was believed to be a boy with red eyes. The warrens have always had their sceptics when it comes to the paranormal but Ed offered three-thousand dollars to prove the case was a hoax, a claim which he later stated no one ever claimed. The warrens also revealed in an interview that the Lutz family members underwent polygraph tests about their experiences and the results showed no indication of deceit.

Doubts and sceptical opinions

- When the Lutz family moved out, the Cromarty family that moved into the house experienced no unusual activity.
- The Cromarty family filed lawsuits against The Lutz family, the book publishers and Jay Anson because of breach of privacy as they were constantly disturbed by paranormal enthusiasts and tourists. The claim was settled for an undisclosed amount.
- The American Society for Psychical Research did not investigate the property as they found the incident questionable.
- There was a claim that the house was built on top of a Native American burial ground, this was dismissed by Native America leaders.
- The priest that was reportedly involved in the case of the haunting stated that he only ever discussed the matter with the family over the telephone.

Chapter Nine: Haunted and Cursed Artefacts

'Sometimes legends make reality and become more
useful than the facts.'
Salman Rushdie

Throughout the world there are thousands of reportedly
haunted or cursed artefacts. In this chapter we will
discover some of the more well-known paranormal
items, their history, and their reported activity let you
decide, are the stories true? Or like most tales are they
created just to keep the legend alive.

The Crying Boy

The Crying Boy is a mass-produced print of a painting
by Giovanni Bragolin which was widely distributed from
the 1950s onwards; there are many variations but the
subject remains the same a portrait of a crying boy or
girl. The curse of The Crying Boy was first documented
by an article in The Sun newspaper in September 1985
that reported the painting would often be found
undamaged in the ruins of burned down houses. The
story of The Crying Boy became so widespread that by
November that same year the newspaper started
organising mass bonfires of the paintings that were been
sent in by its readers. The painting was sent for extensive
testing at the Building Research Establishment where it
was revealed that the paintings were treated with a
varnish that was fire retardant and was the possible

explanation as to the paintings being able to survive the intense fires. Another possible explanation that has been put forth by sceptics is that because the painting is often hung up by the string, the string would often be burned away causing the painting to fall face down on the ground thus giving more protection to the print. On a personal note my grandmother owned a crying boy painting and no fires burned down her house and the picture still remains in the family.

Busby's Chair

This story dates back to the late seventeenth century. Thomas Busby and his father-in-law Daniel Auty ran a very unsuccessful coin counterfeiting business. Busby owned a local inn, was known to love a good drink and was always seen fighting with his father-in-law. The story goes that one day, Busby returned home to find Auty sitting in his favourite chair. Tempers began to flair and one night Busby bludgeoned Auty to death with a hammer and disposed of the body in the woods. When the body was finally discovered, Busby was arrested and charged with his father in laws murder and sentenced to be hanged. On his way to the gallows, it is said he requested to have one final drink in his favourite chair. 'Death would shortly follow those who sat in it' was said to be the words he used to curse the chair. The so-called curse gained modern day infamy when during World War Two where two pilots dared each other to sit in the chair. A week after they sat in the chair, both pilots were killed in a car accident. Other deaths attributed to the chair include a man dying from a heart attack after sitting in the chair, a woman who died from a brain tumour after she bumped into the chair and a young construction worker who sat in the chair falling to his death. Were these deaths a coincidence? Or was it the work of the curse? The chair now has a permanent home in The Thirsk Museum, where it is nailed to the wall so visitors cannot tempt fate and risk the wrath of Busby's Chair.

Koh-I-Noor

The Koh-I-Noor known as 'Mountain of Light' is a diamond that is currently part of the British crown jewels. The diamond was given to Queen Victoria after the annexing of the Punjab in 1849. 'He who owns this diamond will own the world; but will also know its misfortunes. Only God or a woman can wear it with impunity.' These are the words that are said to have formed the curse because of the diamond's bloody history at the hands of men. Queen Victoria decreed in her will that only females of the royal family may wear the diamond.

Robert the Doll

Robert the Doll is a reportedly haunted doll that currently resides at the East Martello Museum. The doll originally belonged to Robert Eugene Otto who was given the doll as a gift from his grandfather on his birthday and was dressed in one of Robert's own childhood clothes. According to reports, Robert has the ability to move, change his facial expressions and has been heard to giggle. It is said those who have seen the doll and made fun of him seem to suffer from misfortunes from job losses, car accidents, broken bones, and even divorces. To this day the museum still receives letters addressed to Robert offering apologies for their disrespect in hopes that this will lift their misfortunes.

Annabelle

Annabelle is perhaps one of the most famous haunted dolls in the world and the inspiration behind the film series of the same name. The doll currently resides at the occult museum that was once owned by demonologist Ed Warren and his wife Lorraine. The story of the doll according to the Warrens is that the doll belonged to a student nurse. The nurse spoke to a psychic when the doll began acting strangely and was told the doll was the host of a spirit called Annabelle and exhibited malicious and frightening behaviour. The Warrens were called in to investigate the doll and announced that the spirit was demonically possessed and agreed to take possession of the doll for safe keeping. They placed the doll behind glass in hopes that this would contain the dolls mischief. So, what do you think? Is the doll really the vessel for a demonic entity or like some sceptics claim, because of the lack of evidence to prove the origins of the doll is it just another tale to encourage visitors to the museum?

Curse of the 'Little Bastard'

Little Bastard was the name that Dean christened his silver Porsche 550 Spyder. It would be the car that leads to his death On September 30, 1955, after a head on collision. Eerily only a week before, Alec Guinness warned Dean Saying 'Please, never get in it. It is now ten o'clock, Friday the 23rd of September 1955. If you get in that car, you will be found dead in it by this time next week.' Dean would not be the last affected by their association with the Little Bastard. George Barris a hot rod designer bought the car planning to sell it for parts. The mechanic whose job it was to dismantle the wreck had his legs crushed when the car fell on top of him. The tires from the Little Bastard that were sold all blew out at the same time causing the driver to be treated in hospital for the injuries they received. The engine was sold to a Dr who was later killed in his own car accident and the transport responsible for hauling the remains of the shell of the Little Bastard was also involved in a crash which ended with the driver being killed. Could the curse of the Little Bastard be true? Or are these just a series of coincidental events?

Uluru Rocks

The Uluru is a large rock formation of sandstone located in Australia; it is also known as Ayers Rock. The structure is regarded as highly sacred to the Anangu Aboriginal people. For year's visitors would climb the rock and take pieces of the structure as a keepsake from their visit to this natural wonder, this was an unwise decision. Over the years various authorities in Australia have reported received packages containing Uluru rocks, with notes of apologies because the sender had been the recipient of bad luck and misfortune, blaming it on a curse.

Chapter Ten: Famous Ghosts

'Those who do not remember the past are condemned to
repeat it.'
George Santayana

Our history has been a long and bloody one, filled with
war, plague, famine and death. It's hardly surprising then
that there have been many reported ghost sightings
throughout history. The question is then, are these
ghostly tales true? Or is it just a great way to attract
tourists and would be ghost hunters, you decide.

The Ghost of Suki

Suki was a sixteen-year-old barmaid at the George &
Dragon pub in West Wycombe. Suki was said to be a
lady of great beauty with many admirers but was said to
have eyes for a handsome stranger. It is said that out of
jealousy three local men forged a note for Suki that was
from the stranger, telling her to meet in the local caves,
wearing a wedding dress. Suki entered the cave to seek
out the man but was greeted by jeering and cruel
laughter. Enraged Suki began to throw rocks at her cruel
jokers only for them to throw rocks back; unfortunately,
one struck Suki and killed her. The men out of fear took
her body back to her room and left it there to be
discovered the next morning. The ghost of Suki is said to
haunt the caves, her old room and the corridors of the

pub. See Chapter Eleven for more information on the caves.

The Welcoming Ghost of The Theatre Royal

There are many ghosts that are said to roam the Theatre Royal at Drury Lane however there is one ghost sighting that is the most intriguing; it is known as the man in grey. The legend of this ghost is that his appearance at a rehearsal is said to be a good omen that a show will be a success. No one knows the true identity of this ghost however, in the 1840s the theatre was undergoing renovations when a skeleton was discovered behind a wall, with a knife in its chest and this is who the spirit is reported to be.

Anne Boleyn

Anne Boleyn, second wife of Henry VIII was sentenced to be beheaded after being found guilty on the charges of adultery, incest and high treason. Her ghost is allegedly seen near the Tower of London, with her head tucked under her arm as she passes the area where she was executed. Her ghost is also said to roam Saint Peters Church where her body was laid to rest and is reported to be appear at Blickling Hall every year on May 19th, the day of her execution.

Catharine Howard

Catharine Howard was the fifth wife of King Henry VIII. She was arrested and charged with committing adultery for which she would be sentenced to death. It is said that during her arrest at Hampton Court, she managed to break free and fled to the Chapel Royal where she believed Henry would be at prayer. She begged Henry for forgiveness and pleaded for her life, but these pleas fell on deaf ears, Catharine was dragged away screaming. The legend goes that her ghostly screams can still be heard at Hampton Court, now known as The Hunted Gallery, where the screams have caused multiple staff and visitors to faint.

John Crossland

John Crossland was a criminal turned executioner who faced a tough decision, to hang for his crimes or be pardoned at the expense of dispensing quick justice to his father and brother. Rather than risk his neck he chose to execute his loved ones. The reason for this unusual choice was because at the time Derby Geol was without an executioner because of the belief that even if you were to take a life in the name of justice your soul would become tainted and unable to ascend to heaven. After the execution he became Derby's most popular executioner and was in high demand until his dying days. The choices that John made seemed to have weighed heavily on him as his ghost is allegedly seen on the church grounds, perhaps seeking forgiveness from those who felt the weight of his axe.

Al Capone and the Ghost of 'Jimmy'

Al Capone, one of the most infamous mobsters of the twentieth century who was allegedly responsible for the Saint Valentine's Day Massacre and co-founder of the Chicago outfit was haunted by an apparition he called 'Jimmy.' For all of the bloodshed that Capone was reportedly responsible for, he was only ever convicted of concealing a concealed weapon and tax evasion. It is during his first stay at Philadelphia's Eastern State Penitentiary that he encountered Jimmy. It was said that it would be a regular nightly occurrence that Capone would be heard screaming for Jimmy to leave him alone. Upon re-entering society, he saw the help of a medium to try and rid him of the tormenting spirit, all attempts to do so would end in failure. The spirit would follow him until the day he died. Who was this spirit? Some claim he was a ghost of one of his victims while others say it was nothing more than a guilty conscience that progressively got worse as syphilis began to spread to his mind, what do you think? Al Capone himself is said to haunt his old cell at Alcatraz, where visitors have claimed to hear the sounds of a ghostly banjo being played.

Lord Brougham and the pact

While not a well-known ghost story, this tale is a rather intriguing one. Lord Brougham made a pact with a fellow student while they were studying at university; they began to discuss the afterlife. The agreement was that whoever died first would appear to the other to settle the discussion. After finishing their time at university, the two men lost contact with Brougham's friend relocating to India and for a time the pact was forgotten about. One evening while Brougham was stepping out of his bath, he was startled to see his friend sitting in the chair across from him. Slightly startled he took note of the date, December 19th. Sometime later, Brougham received a letter from India informing him that his friend had died. The date of his passing? December 19th.

Abraham Lincoln

Abraham Lincoln, the sixteenth president of the United States has long been seen as a ghostly figure around the White House. In one instance he appeared to an aide of President Benjamin Harrison. The aide would hear footsteps and rapping noises follow him with no natural explanation for the phenomena. Scared, the aide would later attend a séance where the ghost of Lincoln allegedly made his presence known. The aide asked, 'Please do not do it again Mr Lincoln, I am now guarding the life of President Harrison now and you've got me scared, I cannot do my duty.' The guard was reportedly never troubled by the spectre again. Perhaps one of the more comical instances that Lincoln has allegedly made an appearance was to Prime Minister Winston Churchill. Churchill was fond of late evening baths. One evening when getting out of the bath, naked with nothing but his cigar he walked into the adjoining room and was taken aback to see Lincoln standing by the fireplace. Churchill known for his wit, flicked his cigar and said ''Good evening, Mr President, you seem to have me at a disadvantage.'' The apparition smiled and then, vanished.

The Drummer of Tedworth

This legend is possibly one of the oldest reported poltergeist cases, dating back to the seventeenth century. The legend takes place in the town of Tedworth, a vagrant called William Drury was down on his luck would bang on his drum in order to bring attention to his situation to passersby who would take pity on him. The Local magistrate, Mompesson however began to grow tired of his constant pestering and disturbances that he made several accusations against the drummer but let him off with a warning with the order that he was to leave town and never return. The only request that William had was for the drum to be returned to him, which Mompesson denied. He decided to keep the drum until he decided what to do with it. Not long after Mompesson left for London to take care of some business matters, upon his return he was surprised to see his wife, rather startled. She began to explain to him the unusual activity that had been taking place at their home. The paranormal activity she allegedly reported included; knocking, scratching sounds and the banging of a drum. The activity only seemed to intensify upon the magistrates return with the drumming sound being heard from places that were inhumanly possible to reach such as the roof. Mompesson had enough and reached out to a local clergyman Reverend Cragg, hoping he would be able expel the spirit. All attempts by Cragg only seemed to intensify the paranormal activity. Finally, Mompesson took matters into his own hands, he had long suspected that all of the activity was the result of the vagrant that he threw out of town and resolved to find him. When Mompesson finally tracked down Drury, he discovered he had been arrested in Gloucester for theft. Drury openly admitted he used witchcraft as an act of revenge on Mompesson because he would not return the drum. It is said that Drury would agree to lift the curse he had placed in return for his innocence at his trial, however this was not to be. He was found guilty and was deported; his fate after leaving the country remains unknown, with some sources claiming he returned many years later to Tedworth, others that he died at sea.

Sir Francis Drake

Sir Francis Drake was a famous English explorer known for his circumnavigation of the world in a single expedition. There are multiple ghost stories linked with

Sir Francis Drake. The first legend is that his ghost inhabits the replica of his drum that is kept at Buckland Abby as is said to drum when England is under attack. The darker legend that surrounds his ghost is that it is said to ride across Dartmoor, in a jet-black coach led by goblins and chased by a pack of vicious dogs. The reason for this legend is because the locals feared Drake, because they believe that to defeat the Spanish Armada, he made a pact with the devil. Some say that this legend is what inspired Sir Arthur Conan Doyle to pen The Hound of the Baskervilles.

The Bell Witch

The Bell Witch was an alleged haunting that took place in the nineteenth century that centred on the Bell family. From 1817-1821 the family and the surrounding area, was the focus of poltergeist activity from an unseen force. Some of the activity reported included unexplained bangs; the sounds of chains rattling and physical attacks on the family. According to the legend, the entity identified itself as Kate Batts, a former neighbour of John Bell who while alive had terrible business dealings with. It is believed that the activity continued until the mysterious death of John Bell, whose body was discovered next to an empty vial of what some believe was poison, after which the activity seemed to settle down. According to paranormal investigators the area of the haunting is still regarded as a paranormal hotspot. The real question with this haunting is that is the story of the haunting real? Or is it an example of how legends can sometimes be mistaken for facts?

The Brown Lady

The Brown Lady is a ghost that reportedly haunts Raynham Hall in Norfolk, England. The ghost is reportedly that of Lady Dorothy Townshend, the second wife of Charles Townshend. The legend goes that Charles believed his wife had committed adultery with another Lord. As punishment, he locked her away in their home where in 1726 she succumbed to smallpox. There are several documented encounters with her spirit, the most famous of which would come in the form of a photograph. In 1936 Hubert C. Provand and his assistant Indre Shira were working for Country Life Magazine taking photographs that would be featured in an article that was being written about Raynham Hall, they had already taken a photograph of the stairs but decided to take another. When the pair came to develop the negatives, they noticed something strange, there was a mist like figure in the shape of a woman on the stairs, the photograph would be printed alongside the article that appeared in Country Life Magazine and thus the legend of the Brown Lady had renewed interest. What makes the case of the Brown Lady more interesting is that renowned ghost hunter Harry Price interviewed the photographers and could find no reason to disbelieve them or that they had used any type of fakery to create the image. Sceptics argue however that trickery could have been used to create the photograph such as grease being applied to the lens or that the figure was simply down to flaws that were commonplace in the cameras of the time which were prone to problems such as double exposure. The validity of the photograph is still hotly debated today.

Did you know that several colours have long been associated with reported sightings of ghosts? No one fully understands why these apparitions have these unusually appearances however they are usually female and believed to have died in traumatic ways, here are some examples:

Red Lady

A Lady in Red is said to be attributed to a jilted lover or prostitutes killed in fits of passion. These ghosts are reportedly seen wearing scarlet or blood-stained clothes and are said to haunt locations such as hotels, theatres or public places. A Red Lady is reported to haunt Ghostlight theatre in New York.

White Lady

A lady in white is attributed to legends of accidental death, murder, suicide and general feelings of loss. A White Lady has reportedly been seen running across the Beeford Straight towards the junction of North Frodingham.

Green Lady

The Green lady is sometimes associated with legends of drowning and suicide, A green lady has reportedly been seen at Firbeck Hall, Yorkshire. The legend goes that she drowned herself after her roundhead lover was killed.

Bonnie and Clyde

The tale of Bonnie and Clyde is perhaps one of the most romanticised stories of criminals ever told. During the 1930s they, along with their gang terrorised Central America they were reportedly responsible for at least thirteen murders and their list of crimes included bank robberies, burglaries and kidnappings. When the police finally caught the gang on a road in Bienville Parish, Louisiana they reportedly fired around one hundred and fifty shots, Clyde was killed instantly with Bonnie dying shortly after. It should be no surprise then that their spirits are said to be seen at the site where they were gunned down. Visitors to the Whiskey Pete's Hotel and Casino in Primm, Nevada where their bullet riddled car is on display have also claimed to have strange experiences when near the car, some claiming to feel eerily cold and others claiming to see strange anomalies on pictures they have taken of the car.

Chapter Eleven: Haunted Locations

'I think that everybody should go out there and test their
curiosity, find a haunted place.'
Zak Bagans

Around the world, there are locations that have had
numerous documented experiences with the paranormal.
In this chapter you will discover some of these places in
hopes that this will inspire you to do some research for
yourself about the locations, perhaps even visit them.
Will you have an experience of your own? Or will you
be the one to dispel some of the ghost stories that
associated with them.

Ancient Ram Inn

The Ancient Ram Inn was built in 1145 and is believed
to be the haunted by as many as twenty spirits. The Inn
is not only built on a pagan burial ground, where bones
are still being uncovered The Inn is also situated on one
of the UKs main Ley lines. Ley lines are allegedly linked
to increased paranormal activity at locations that they
run through. Could these be the reasons the Inn is so
haunted? The ghosts that allegedly haunt the Inn include.

- A witch that was burned at the stake after being
  captured by local witch hunters while she was
  seeking refuge at the Inn.

- A murdered young girl who is believed to be called Rose.

- An Incubus and a Succubus are believed to visit visitors during their sleep. An Incubus is an alleged male demon who lies with sleeping woman in order to have sexual encounters with them. A Succubus is a demon that appears in female form in order to seduce men in their dreams.

The Inn has been visited by many paranormal investigators over the years including the Most Haunted and Ghost Adventure teams where a variety of evidence has been collected. The site was also investigated by the oldest paranormal research organisation in the world, The Ghost Club who investigated the pub in 2003 but found no evidence of activity that they considered paranormal.

Epping Forest

Epping Forest back in the 18th century was a very dangerous place to get lost. The forest was reportedly a hideout used by thieves, murderers and highwayman, one of the most famous being Dick Turpin. It should be no surprise then that Turpin's ghost and that of his victims are said to still haunt the woods. One reported example of a residual haunting taking place in the woods comes from the 1920s where there was a report that two friends cycling through the woods began to hear the sounds of an approaching horse and carriage. The men pulled into the side to allow them to pass, however when they looked towards the direction of the sounds, they could see nothing approach, even as the sounds got louder. The men were understandably quite startled and quickly continued on their way. The woods are also said to be the home of a cursed lake. The lake is said to be the site of a murder-suicide of two young lovers over three hundred years ago and is said to draw people to their deaths.

Leap Castle

Leap Castle is a castle in Coolderry, Ireland and is reportedly the most haunted castle in the world; it possibly gained this reputation because of its long and bloody history. The castle was once the seat of the O'Carroll clan. In 1532 a bitter dispute was said to be taking place within the clan which lead one brother to plunge a dagger into another brother's heart, a priest while he was giving mass in the chapel. This act would forever taint the chapel and it would come to be known as The Bloody Chapel. It is said that the ghost of the O'Carroll priest still wonders the chapel. In 1922 workmen discovered a hidden dungeon behind one of the chapel walls. While searching the dungeon the workmen discovered pits filled with wooden spikes and remains of the poor souls who had been placed upon them. Could these poor souls still haunt the chapel? The Castle is allegedly home to children ghosts as well. According to several psychics two girls called Emily and Charlotte are sisters. Charlotte has allegedly been seen running up and down the castles spiral staircase. It is believed this is because Emily Died after falling from the castle tower and Charlotte is still searching for her. Finally, the Castle is reportedly haunted by a powerful entity known as The Elemental. An elemental is a term used to describe an entity that was neither human nor demonic and is often associated with the practice of witchcraft. The Elemental has many different stories attached to it but one theory is that Elder Druids summoned the entity on land where castle was built, to protect the area from harm.

Paris Catacombs

The Paris catacombs are underground ossaries that reportedly hold the remains of over six million people. The catacombs history dates back to the eighteenth century when Paris' cemeteries were overflowing. The decision was made that Charles-Axel Guillaumot who was King Louis XVI architect, would be given the monumental task to relocate the older remains of those interred in these cemeteries and to relocate them to a mine in Rue de la Tombe-Issoire, a task which would take twelve years to complete. The walls of the mine would become lined with the bones of the dead and the tunnels are believed to extend over two-hundred miles. Could this desecration of the remains be the cause of the supposed hauntings linked to the caves? One of the ghosts that is said to haunt the caves is Philibert Apsairt. Philibert was a doorman for the Val-de-Grâce hospital. It is believed that while he was fetching wine from the cellar he got lost and wound up in the catacombs. Unfortunately for him he only had a small candlelight and once it blew out, he became lost and died, his remains went undiscovered for eleven years.

Pendle Hill

Pendle Hill is allegedly haunted by the spirit of at least ten witches who were hung at Lancaster castle and were buried beneath the hills. All of the witches that were accused were all denied access to legal council and the right to call witnesses, could this injustice be the reason that the witches are said to still haunt the hills? The witches are not the only ones who are said to haunt the hills, there have been stories of phantom travellers being seen on the hills who are believed to be the spirits of those who have lost their way.

Renishaw Hall

Renishaw Hall is a beautiful country house in Renishaw, Derbyshire. The house was built in 1625 by George Sitwell who became High Sheriff of Derbyshire in 1653. The location has multiple ghost sighting associated with it. Women who visit the hall report being kissed on the hand and touched by an unseen entity; local legends claim this to be the boy in pink who was believed to be a boy in his young teens that died while staying at the hall. A servant girl is also reportedly seen in the corridors heading towards where an old staircase was located, only to vanish at what would have been the base of the staircase. Finally, there is a monk that is claimed to walk the grounds of Renishaw, those who have tried to call attention to the monk are said to see him vanish soon after their sighting.

The Hellfire Caves

The Hellfire Caves in West Wycombe is a man-made structure excavated by Sir Francis Dashwood between 1748 and 1752. The caves are so named because of their association with the Hellfire Club. The club reportedly took part in rituals and sacrifices which could be the reason why the caves have so much paranormal activity. The caves are allegedly haunted by several ghosts the first of which is a former steward of Dashwood called Paul Whitehead. Whitehead reportedly left his heart to Dashwood in his will requesting that it be kept in an urn in the caves. At some point in time his heart was stolen from the urn and this is believed to be what caused the haunting. His spirit has apparently been seen roaming the caves searching for his lost heart, unable to find rest until it is returned. Another Ghost that is said to haunt the caves is Suki, who we discussed in the previous chapter.

The Old Fire Station Museum

The Old Fire Station Museum is a building that was constructed in 1897 and housed the police, fire and ambulance services in Sheffield, South Yorkshire. The building was retired from service in 1965 and housed a variety of tenants until it was taken over by South Yorkshire Fire Services Historical Society in 1984 with the aim of turning the building into a museum. One of the ghosts that are frequently seen in the building is an old fireman who wanders the old building and allegedly interacts with the visitors who often mistake him for someone who works at the museum. Another residential ghost is believed to haunt the building is a spirit who identifies himself to mediums as Cain. Cain is said to be a former prisoner who enjoys making his presence felt to visitors, though his spirit is said to be easily angered however, especially if someone enters what is believed to be his old cell.

The Skirrid Mountain Inn

The Skirrid Inn is reportedly one of the oldest inns in Wales with some believe has a very chequered past. There is an old oak beam atop of the stairs with a rope; the reason for this is that the inn was reportedly used as a court of law where capital punishment would be met out. While the rope may not be original the beam serves as a reminder of its past and is perhaps the reason for the entire residual hauntings taking place at the inn. Some of the activity people have reported at the inn includes disembodied voices and screams, poltergeist activity such as moving objects and sudden, extreme temperature drops. Some of the ghosts that haunt the inn include Fanny Price, a former barmaid who died of consumption, a smell of lavender is said to be a sign of her presence. Though history shows no record of any attachment to the inn, psychics have often claimed that the infamous judge George Jeffreys who was known for his part in the Bloody Assizes is linked in some way to the inn.

Winchester Mystery House

Winchester Mystery House is perhaps one of the most well-known haunted houses in America. The house originally belonged to and Sarah Winchester, who married William Winchester, son of the American rifle inventor Oliver Winchester. Upon the passing of her husband, she attempted to contact him through the use of séances but was unsuccessful until she met a medium called Adam Coons. Coons claimed to have made contact with her husband who said that she was under a curse and that all of the spirits killed by Winchester rifle caused his death and that of their child and in order to break the curse she must appease the spirits. Believing that Coon was speaking to her husband she sold her house and moved west to Santa Clara Valley to begin what would be The Winchester Mystery House. The building itself is believed to be designed to confuse and contain the spirits that allegedly haunt the property, with stairways and doorways that lead to nowhere, could this be an attempt to build passageways to the spirit world to free the spirits that haunted the property? Each room had thirteen windows, thirteen lights and thirteen closets however there are no mirrors in the house. This was allegedly a request from the ghosts that haunted Sarah Winchester. This may be due to the superstition that if the mirrors in the house of the recently deceased weren't covered up the mirror would trap their soul within them. Visitors to the house have reported paranormal phenomena including disembodied footsteps, cold spots and strange smells.

Ye Olde Trip to Jerusalem

Ye Olde Trip to Jerusalem is reportedly the oldest pub in England and if the stories are true, one of Nottingham's most haunted inns. The inn was reportedly established in 1189 AD; however, there is no documented proof to this claim. The inn supposedly comes from a tale that Ye Olde Trip To Jerusalem would be the last stop for recruits before they went to fight in the crusades. The inn is home to an alleged cursed object, known as 'The Galleon.' The legend surrounding the item is that it was given as payment for an outstanding tab or was given as a gift by a passing sailor. The Galleon is allegedly responsible for the deaths of at least three people, all of whom had cleaned it, coincidence or curse? The item is now encased in a glass cabinet so that no one else will try to tempt fate. The old cellars of the inn are also said to be rife with paranormal activity. The cellars are linked to the castle and would have been used to house prisoners when the jail was overflowing. Disembodied voices, screams and footsteps have reportedly been heard in these areas. Could this be prisoners who died down there causing paranormal activity? Or is it simply just our own echoes that are reverberating off the natural rock caves?

Chapter Twelve: How to Create a Ghost

'No amount of belief makes something fact'
James Randi

For years there have been numerous attempts by research societies to try to understand what would lead us to believe in the existence of the paranormal. It has led to numerous theories to be published on subjects ranging from near death experiences to telepathy, despite this it seems that even in the twenty-first century we are still no closer to understanding the paranormal. In 1972 a group of researchers based in Toronto decided to try and see if they could connect with a spirit of a different kind.

The Philip Experiment

In 1972 the Toronto Society for Psychical Research conducted and experiment to see if they could contact a spirit called Philip, using an Ouija Board. This may not seem unusual as experiments such as this are conducted by research facilities all the time, however with this experiment there was a twist, the entity called Philip was completely fictional. The research team was led by Dr A.R George Owen and consisted of his wife his wife Lorne, engineer Al Peacock, accountant Bernice M, bookkeeper Dorothy O'Donnell, sociology student Sidney K, designer Andy H and a former chairperson of MENSA Margaret Sparrow. Together the group created a fictional profile and biography of a man they called

Philip Aylesford. If you would like to read the biography it can be found here; https://www.liveabout.com/how-to-create-a-ghost-2594058. The initial tests that the group conducted yielded no results and the team began to believe the experiment has failed. The decision was made that they should try to simulate the atmosphere that you would encounter at a traditional séance, the lights were dimmed and soon after they began, the group started to feel as if they were receiving paranormal activity. The activity the group recorded included table vibrations, rapping noises and receiving relevant responses in regard to questions about Philip's life, the only activity that the team had hoped for and did not receive was a physical manifestation of Philip. The group considered the experiment a success, so much so that the decision was made to see if the results could be replicated with a different group of individuals. The second group seemed to replicate the results of the original experiment with the exception fictional spirit called Lilith, a French-Canadian spy. So how was it done? Dr Owens believed that the participants activated a subconscious defence mechanism that presented itself in the form of paranormal activity. The results may have also been down to the group's expectations and their will for something to happen, especially when you consider they only started to receive activity when they changed the conditions to mimic that of a traditional séance and this would subconsciously create the expectation for activity to occur. The experiments are believed to be what inspired the films The Apparition and The quiet Ones.

This would not be the only time that a fictional experiment would have unexpected results. In 1992 Stephen Volk pitched an idea to the BBC that would change the lives of many and not always for the better, that project was called Ghostwatch.

Ghostwatch

Ghostwatch was a 1992 pseudo-documentary which aired on the BBC on Halloween night and was watched by 11 million viewers. The film was shot in the style of a live special investigation with one segment taking place at a house in London where poltergeist activity had been reported and a studio segment that featured Michael Parkinson and a paranormal expert Dr Lin Pascoe discussing the investigation and attempting to explain the unusual events that had taken place in the house. Throughout the evening interview footage of the neighbours and the family who lived in the house was played in which they discuss the paranormal activity and discover that it is being caused by the ghost of Pipes. The ghost of Pipes was said to be the spirit of Raymond Tunstall a psychologically disturbed man who was believed to have suffered a haunting himself, by the ghost of Mother Seddons, a child killer from the 19th century. At one point during the night, one of the children was caught banging the pipes in an attempt to persuade the investigators that the activity occurring at the house was real, after the child was caught Parkinson dismissed the whole incident as a hoax but Dr Lin wasn't so sure. During the program viewers were encouraged to call in to discuss their own experiences on what was occurring, most of the activity reported by viewers seemed to be related to the program itself and the activity seemed to get worse as the show progressed. The opinion is put forward by Dr Lin that the broadcast has been acting like a national séance and through this action the poltergeist Pipes was gaining tremendous energy. It is at this point that the paranormal activity becomes extremely dangerous, host Sarah Greene is seen being dragged by unseen forces behind a door and then begins to affect the BBC studios and transmitter causing the studio lights to explode leaving the studio in complete darkness. In the end all viewers can hear is Parkinson being possessed and speaking a nursery rhyme in Pipes' voice, "Fee, Fi, Fo, Fum..."

How it was done

The show was in fact recorded weeks in advance and was formatted and presented as if it was a live broadcast and 'live' calls were timed to coincide with the paranormal activity happening on screen. There were so many calls to the BBC switchboard that it overloaded the system and many viewers were greeted with the engaged tone meaning they did not hear the pre-recorded message assuring fans that the program was fictionalised and encouraging them to share their own ghost stories. This occurrence helped to sell the illusion that what was being witnessed on screen were true, an unintentional affect but certainly effective.

The Aftermath of Ghostwatch

- The BBC was inundated with phone calls from frightened viewers believing the show to be factual.

- The BBC was heavily criticised by the media for its portrayal of disturbing scenes, even though the show aired after the watershed.

- The broadcasting standards commission stated in a ruling 'The BBC had a duty to do more than simply hint at deception that it was practicing on the audience and that there was a deliberate attempt to cultivate a sense of menace.

- In February 1994 there was a published report in the British Medical Journal that described two cases of Ghostwatch inducted post-traumatic stress disorder in two ten-year-old boys.

- Ghostwatch is partially what Derren Brown used to create his special 'Séance'

Originally, I was going to incorporate my own version of Ghostwatch into this book in the form of a report that would have documented a fictional investigation. The case would have involved the haunting of a location by three spirits called Alfie Kalts, Fran Tudule and Rob Suttellock. For those with an inquisitive mind you may have noticed that these are anagrams, if you would like to know what they are you will find them in the glossary section.

Chapter Thirteen: Explanations for Paranormal Activity

'How much of the paranormal relies on perception?'
Sarah Haywood

For as long as there has been evidence of the paranormal there have also been numerous ways to explain them, but sometimes no matter how hard you try to put forward an explanation you will never be able to change someone's opinion on the paranormal. So, tell me dear reader, are these explanations the cause of paranormal activity? Or is it just someone's way to try and rationalise the unexplained.

Pareidolia

Have you ever looked up at a cloud and thought 'that cloud looks like a sheep? This is an example of the pareidolia effect. Pareidolia is the tendency to incorrectly identify random patterns or shapes and attributing them to something else. The most common use of this effect is in the field of psychology. A psychologist will sometimes show their patients pictures in the form of ink blocks and ask them what they see. Their answer helps provide insight to a person's psyche however the method isn't widely recognised as an accurate way to diagnose a patient. Pareidolia is what some researchers attribute to rational explanations of paranormal activity. Below I have listed some examples as to how this effect works.

- Our eyes often register shapes to be humanoid, so sometimes we may see figures where indeed there are none.

- Specks of dust or bugs may appear to us as orbs simply because our eyes do not have enough time to focus on them before they disappear.

- From certain angles when taking pictures, patterns on the wall can appear to be facial features.

- Pareidolia doesn't just apply to the things we see but also to what we hear, EVPs for example are quite susceptible to this effect. The reason for this is because we will interpret sounds that we hear for words because our minds are trying to process it and the more we hear that sound the more likely we are to believe that is the words that we heard.

To show how pareidolia can affect your EVP evidence here is an interesting experiment you can try for yourselves, all you require are a group of friends and a digital recorder. Make a recording of yourself saying something in a muffled voice saying several phrases, for example 'hello there' then follow these instructions.

Test 1: Controlled Conditions

Have your friends listen to the recording one by one not allowing them to interact with the other participants and have them write down what they think is being said and put it in a glass and get them to go into another room to the rest of the group so they cannot influence someone else's answer. After all the participants have written down a response, look at the answers to see if a consensus has been reached.

Test 2: Conformation Bias Suggestion

Follow the same stages as above but while playing the EVP place a suggestion to the listener as to what it is you believe is being said and see if you can influence their answer.

Test 3: Group Conformation Bias Suggestion

For the final session gather all the participants together and play the EVP to them. Allow the group to discuss the recording and then get them to place their answer on a piece of paper and place it in a glass. And then look at the results. If the experiment worked in the way I thought it would, you should see a majority of the same answers.

Ideomotor Phenomena

Ideomotor Phenomena is a psychological effect where a person makes movement subconsciously. It comes from the Latin words 'ideo' meaning idea and 'moto' meaning muscular action. It is believed by scientists and sceptics of the paranormal that items such as dowsing rods, Ouija boards, pendulums and automatic writing all rely heavily on input from this phenomenon in order to produce results. In a study from 2019 on automatic pendulum movements a motion system showed that the pendulum moved while the fingers were holding it. This study showed that the resonant frequency in the pendulum was close to that oscillating frequency causing movement in the pendulum. You can see the Ideomotor Phenomena yourself all it requires is some string and a weighted down object like a ring. Hold out your arm keeping it as still as possible and hold the string and you will see that the more you concentrate the more likely there will be movement.

The Backscatter Effect

Many people at some point in their life will have seen some form of orb whether that is in person, on film or in a photograph. Orbs are believed by some to be the first physical manifestation of a ghost; however, there is a more logical explanation. Backscatter is an optical phenomenon that results in circular distortions on images captured by a camera flash being reflected from dust, water droplets, insects and other particles in the air or off reflected surfaces. Due to these numerous explanations, most researchers do not consider orbs as evidence of the paranormal because there as so many natural explanations like the backscatter effect.

You can see for yourself how this effect can create the illusion of orbs, all you need is a camera some talcum powder and a reflective surface such as a window. Point the camera towards the reflective surface, release a small amount of talcum powder into the atmosphere and take a couple of photographs and review the pictures. The results you have captured should replicate the appearance of orbs; this experiment should also produce similar results with a film camera.

Natural Occurring Phenomena

Have you ever noticed that a lot of these haunted locations are run down, half destroyed or quite literally falling apart? These conditions can go a long way to explaining paranormal activity.

- Falling debris could be the cause of stones being 'thrown'.

- Black mould is believed to have an effect on a person psychologically such as hallucinations the longer someone is exposed to it.

- Empty building means there will be echoing, so phantom footsteps and voices could just be that of your own.

- Natural temperature changes, as a building cools down or warms up naturally the structure of the building can cause creaking within the woodwork.

- A person's state of mind. If a person has recently lost someone then they would be more susceptible to suggestion of seeing or hearing phenomena. Also linked to this is confirmation bias, where you hear what you want to hear or you hear something that will confirm your belief.

Chapter Fourteen: Faiths, Ghosts and Exorcisms

'To one who has faith, no explanation is necessary. To
one without faith, no explanation is possible.'
Thomas Aquinas

The paranormal and religions are not something you
would consider coinciding, but why not? Take
Christianity for example, Jesus somehow performed
miracle healing techniques by using the laying on of
hands to heal a blind mind according to the gospel of
Mark. He performed exorcisms on people to rid them of
demons and spirits that possessed them and was even
resurrected on the seventh day after his crucifixion,
would we not consider these actions as paranormal
today? Exorcism, derives from the Greek word
ἐξορκισμός meaning binding by oath, is a religious
practice used to drive out demonic or spiritual entities
from a person or location. Each faith has its own views
on the paranormal and exorcisms and so in this chapter
we shall discuss how some faiths deal with these issues.

Christianity

Christianity is considered the world's largest religion
with it 2.8 billion followers in over 257 countries and
territories. Christians follow the teaching of Jesus Christ,
the Messiah and son of God. In regard to ghosts,
Christians are taught that it is sinful to conjure or control
spirits. According to Deuteronomy XVIII 'You must not

cast spells or ask spirits for help or consult the dead, whoever does these things is disgusting to our Lord.' It is also stated in Timothy 4:1 that ghosts are actually demons in disguise. Some Christian denominations also believe that ghosts are beings that linger in an intermediate state, before going onto heaven. From my perspective, to say you should not do these things, when Jesus was able to rise from the dead to speak to his followers after his crucifixion and was perform healing miracles could seem rather hypocritical, as surly he would have been viewed as a spirit?

In Christianity, an exorcism is performed on an individual or place in order to cast out negative and demonic entities, the ceremony is conducted by and individual known as an exorcist. Exorcists are often high-ranking individuals within their church who are graced with special knowledge and equipment needed to carry out the ritual. Before an exorcism is performed, permission must be sought by not only someone close to the person who may require the rite of exorcism but also from higher authorities within the church. For example, in Catholicism, it must be authorised first by the local bishops and only after natural explanations have been ruled out such as issues with mental health. If the exorcism is being performed on an individual, they are generally restrained in order to protect them and those conducting the ritual. During the exorcism, the priest will often invoke the name of God and Jesus in order to drive out the entities, while also quoting from the bible,

115

spraying Holy water and burning incense in order to purify the space.

Islam

Islam is considered the second largest religion with over 1.9 billion followers worldwide. Islam teaches us that God is merciful and unique and guides humanity through spiritual scriptures and prophets. The primary scripture in Islam is known as the Quran which is believed to be the word of God that was revealed orally to his final Prophet Muhammad through the archangel Gabriel.

In Islam the souls of the dead dwell in Barzakh, meaning separation or barrier. It is a place that separates the dead from the living. In some instances, it is believed that dead can appear to us, these spirits are either saints or impure souls. In Islam, some exorcisms are performed by a Sheikh who places their hand atop of the head of the possessed and will recite verses from the Quran, specifically ones that invoke the help of God. Holy water from the Zamzam Well is sprinkled around the possessed. Following these processes can help expel the tormenting spirits which are usually referred to as Jinn. Jinn are believed to be intelligent spirits lower in rank than angels that can appear in different forms and can possess humans.

Spiritualism

Spiritualism is a religious movement based on a belief that the spirits of the departed have a natural ability to interact and communicate with the living. Spiritualists believe that once we die, part of our personality survives and exists as part of the spirit plane. There are reportedly over 326 affiliated spiritualist churches around the world. Spiritualists claim that mediums can be used to bridge the connection between our world and that of spirit world in order to pass on messages from the deceased. March 31st, 1848, is considered to have special meaning, as many consider it the birth of the movement. It is on that day that the Fox sisters claim to have made contact with a murdered peddler.

While Spiritualist churches do not necessarily deal with exorcism, some churches towards the end of every meeting will conduct a healing circle. A healing circle is a practice where the participants will hold hands and share their collective energy towards someone in the group who requires it. This could include someone who feels they are being repressed by negative energies.

I personally attended some spiritualist churches in my late teenage years and can say that the whole experience is a strange one. Being surrounded by people who believe in this faith singing psalms, to see the hope in the people's eyes hoping to receive a message was a heart-warming sensation, however when it came to listening to their guest medium, I was most of the times less impressed. Personally, I believe that they were using simple cold reading techniques or that because mediums belonging to the faith actually travel from church to church, they may have remembered past readings they had given. There was one time however that a medium may have actually had genuine information for me. I had grown tired of the consistent cold reading and was sat crossed armed, to a medium I must have looked quite standoffish however he proceeded to point me out and gave me a reading. The information he gave to me, relating to a man named John, didn't mean much to me at the time, and the fact that the medium couldn't pinpoint the information without asking if the person was alive or in spirit didn't do much to cement my belief. The medium passed on the message and said I should research the information. I did and to my astonishment it related to my paternal grandfather who died long before I was born. Was this a genuine spiritual encounter or was it an attempt to close me off in case he was wrong? Personally I think it was the latter.

Buddhism

Buddhism is it is the fourth largest faith in the world that was established by Siddhartha Gautama over 2500 years ago in India. Followers of Buddhism focus on trying to achieve enlightenment of the mind, body and soul rather than acknowledging a god or deity. Karma is one of the strongest principles in Buddhism. It is the belief that if a person performs good deeds, this creates good karma whereas if someone performs a bad deed, it creates bad karma. Some believe that the concept of karma plays out a huge part in a soul's rebirth and that our karma in life will determine what we will become in our next life.

In Buddhism it is believed that there are many planes of existence, one of which is known as the realm of Hungry ghost. Hungry ghosts are created from the evil deeds that a person may have committed in life which causes them to be reborn in this form. Is this the Buddhist version of a poltergeist? A Buddhist exorcism is generally performed by a temple's chief priest. The priest will read from scriptures of Buddhism and burn incense (which is possibly sage or frankincense) and perhaps most interestingly, carry a wooden staff embroiled with metal rings that creates sounds to scare off the spirit who is in control of the possessed and to ward off further attacks.

Paganism

I will state that this is my own interpretation of paganism as the practice is so widespread that there are many different viewpoints and beliefs within it. To me is the beauty of it, you can follow your own path and still learn along the way.

Paganism is a term that was originally used by early Christian's worshipers to describe those who help beliefs in 'false Gods.' It should be noted however that most of the pagan concepts were absorbed by Christianity to fulfil their own beliefs. Examples of this include Yule, which Christians would come to call Christmas to represent the birth of Jesus Christ and Ostara which would become Easter and represent the crucifixion and resurrection of Christ. Pagans generally follow the Wheel of the Year which denotes when each new season would start. The wheel consists of eight Sabbats which are Samhain, Yule, Imbolc, Ostara, Beltane, Litha, Lughnasadh and Mabon. Here we shall be focusing more on Samhain or as many of you would know it, Halloween. Samhain is a festival that is held to mark the end of the harvest season; it is during this time that huge bonfires would be lit to honour the old gods and our ancestors. During Samhain, the ghosts of the deceased kin would return seeking refuge and this is why a space would be left at the Samhain feast. Samhain is perhaps one of the most spiritual events to take place as the connection between this world and what lies beyond is strongest because the veil that separates them is at its thinnest.

While there are not really exorcisms is paganism there are several ways which practitioners can protect themselves not just negative energy, but negative people as well. There are a variety of crystals that once charged can offer protection, these include Hematite, Bloodstone, Chlorite and Fluorite. These crystals can be worn to protect the wearer or even placed in a protection grid or placed around thresholds of a location to repel negative energies. The practitioner can also draw runes to provide a protection to them or to a location. Some pagans even use herbs as a method to provide protection; these herbs can be mixed together and placed in pouches which are then placed in different areas of the home. For example, you could place an herb pouch under your mattress to help prevent nightmares. Finally, there is the practice known as sage smudging. The practice of sage smudging has long been used it paganism, it may look similar to an exorcism however it is more of a practice to rid oneself of and home of negative energies rather than driving out evil spirits.

Chapter Fifteen: Paranormal Believers

'Change the way you look at things and the things you
look at will change.'
Wayne W Dyer

In this chapter we will discuss some of the most famous
paranormal believers from the past and the present.
Some you may know; others may surprise you and
perhaps knowing that they are believers will change your
perspective on the paranormal? Or cement your current
opinion.

Sir Arthur Conan Doyle

That's right; the creator of one of the world's most
famous sleuths was a staunch believer in the paranormal
and one of its most ardent defenders, and often described
spiritualism as 'The most important thing in the world.'
In 1889 Doyle became one the founding members of the
Hampshire Society for Psychological Research and
joined the Society for Psychological Research in 1893.
During a meeting with Houdini, Doyle and his wife Jean
who used automatic writing to pass on messages from
the spirit world suggested that they should hold a séance.
Houdini who while sceptical of those who claimed to
contact spirits remained open minded on the subject
agreed as he always wanted to receive a message from
his beloved mother. Jean passed messages onto Houdini
who remained sceptical as the messages which were

passed on were all in English, a language which his mother did not speak and the fact there was no mention that the séance was held on her birthday. Houdini kept his thoughts to himself for several months before giving his thoughts to Doyle. Doyle put forward the argument that it was in English because the two worlds produced a natural translating effect and thus it would be the language of the medium and not the spirit. The incident and Houdini's constant vigils against those who falsely claimed they could contact the dead through trickery and deceit would lead to a rift between the two men that would never be repaired. Houdini died in 1926, never rekindling the friendship that they once had. This is not the only story of his beliefs possibly affecting his judgement. In 1922 Harry Price wrote that spirit photographer William Hope was a fraud, Doyle defended Hope and threatened to have Price removed from the National Laboratory of Psychical Research. Doyle's most famous case would be that of the Cottingley Fairies with we shall cover in chapter twelve. Doyle would go on to write two volumes of books entitled 'The history Of Spiritualism' which led to him being considered one of the most knowledgeable and leading spiritualists of his time.

Zak Bagans

'I never believed in ghost until I came face to face with one' a quote that most Ghost Adventures fans will be familiar with. Originally, like most people, Zak was a sceptic of the paranormal, until one morning he awoke to see a ghostly figure sitting on the edge of his bed. His experience led him to team up with two other like-minded individuals Nick Groff and Aaron Goodwin, to film a one-off documentary which explored their search for proof of the afterlife. In the documentary, they caught a brick being thrown but could not ascertain a logical explanation for the activity. This evidence led to the travel channel offering the men the opportunity to expand their search for proof of the supernatural. Zak's experience has led him to venture around the world in order to find definitive proof of the paranormal. Some of the Ghost Adventures best evidence includes.

- A teddy bear, moving on its own in the Edinburgh Vaults.

- In the episode 'Ireland's Celtic Demons' there are several EVPs that are captured that have no natural explanation including that of a woman saying 'no' when it's an all-male cast and they stopped in the middle of nowhere.

- In the episode 'Hell Hole Prison' with the use of an SLS camera the crew capture a stick figure that appears to dance and a band apparently playing.

In 2017 he opened a 'haunted museum' in Las Vegas which is reportedly filled with artefacts he has collected throughout the years as well as those given to him.

Ed & Lorraine Warren

Ed and Lorraine Warren are two of the most famous paranormal investigators of the modern age and founders of the New England Society for Psychic Research. Edward was a self-taught demonologist and his wife was said to be a light trance medium. The couple claimed to have investigated over 10,000 cases throughout their career. Their most notable cases include The Annabelle Doll, The Amityville Haunting, The Enfield Poltergeist and A Haunting in Connecticut. Most of the cases that have been investigated by the Warrens were the inspirations for several film series.

John Zaffis

John Zaffis is a paranormal researcher known for his series Haunted Collector where he leads a team of paranormal investigators in order to locate causes of hauntings at locations and remove the items responsible for the activity. Zaffis was originally a sceptical when it came to the paranormal until he had an experience where he saw and apparition appear to him at the foot of his bed when he was a teenager. This would lead to an obsession to understanding the paranormal. He spent the first few years learning from his aunt and Uncle Ed and Lorraine Warren and it was their interest in demonology that would lead Zaffis to study the subject himself. Zaffis owns a museum which houses all of the haunted artefacts those he has helped and has collected himself throughout his career.

Chapter Sixteen: Paranormal Sceptics

'That which can be asserted without evidence, can be
dismissed without evidence.'
Christopher Hitchens

For every believer in the paranormal there will always be
a sceptic to offer a differing opinion. A sceptic according
to the Oxford dictionary is 'a person who usually doubts
that claims or statements are true, especially those that
other people believe in.' this is not to say that all sceptics
have the same viewpoint. Some sceptics will only
require proof that there is evidence in the paranormal,
others will question and review evidence before putting
forth an opinion and then there are those who out right
believe there is no such thing as paranormal and that
claims of such can be explained with logical reason and
thought.

Harry Houdini

Harry Houdini was a Hungarian born American
illusionist and stunt performer who was famed for his
daring and risky escape attempts which included The
Chinese water torture cell, the milk can escape and the
buried alive stunt. In the 1920s Houdini began to use his
many years of magical and escape skills towards
uncovering fraudulent psychics and mediums. Houdini
would often attend séances in disguise with an
undercover police officer and once he worked out how

the mediums were being duplicitous inform the officer on the deceit. Houdini was part of a group Scientific American, who would offer a cash reward for definitive proof of the paranormal, the reward went unclaimed. His beliefs about the paranormal would lead to the breakdown of his friendship with believer and spiritualist Sir Arthur Conan Doyle. Doyle held the opinion that Houdini himself was a powerful medium and his great escapes were due to his paranormal abilities and he was using his power to block the spiritual power of those he would set out to debunk. Houdini's greatest illusion was that before he died, he and his wife, a believer in the paranormal, agreed keywords that would allow him to indeed prove there was an afterlife. If indeed there was a medium that was able to connect with him, they would speak the phrase 'Rosabelle believe.' Arthur Ford, founder of the first spiritualist church in New York was renowned for his mediumistic skills and apparently contacted Bess claiming that her husband had contacted him with the codeword's. Bess agreed to meet with Ford and he did indeed confirm this to her however his efforts were denounced by Houdini's friend Joseph Dunninger who claimed that Ford had only guessed the codeword's because it had appeared in a biography about Houdini two years prior to his death. It was eventually discovered that the reason Fords medium skills were so accurate was after he died it was discovered he had collected extensive information on those he would read for, giving him the appearance he was genuine. Ten years after his passing and after one final unsuccessful attempt to connect to her husband, Bess blew out a candle that she kept beside his picture and remarked 'Ten years is long enough to wait for any man.'

In 1926 Houdini went to testify before a congress subcommittee to put forward a bill that would impose a $250 fine or a six-month prison sentence for 'Any person pretending to tell fortunes for rewards or compensation.' Houdini presented his case through his facts that he had collected along with his investigators of as he claimed 'blatant falsehoods' and even presented a list of names of those who had lost vast fortunes on the words of mediums. He wasn't without his critics as he presented his findings to the subcommittee as there were numerous mediums, psychics and spiritualists who had turned up to protest the beliefs which would only antagonise Houdini. To rebuff the group of defenders he threw a crumpled piece of paper and declared to the onlookers to prove him wrong and show him genuine psychic abilities and read what was on the paper, there were no takers and despite his impassioned presentation, the bill was never passed. Perhaps the one strange event to come from this display was Madame Marcia, a prominent psychic and some believe advisor to some of the most powerful people in America claimed that Houdini would be dead by November, he died 31st October 1926, coincidence? or tragic fate?

Rose Mackenberg

Rose Mackenberg was an American investigator who started out as a stenographer. In the 1920s she sought the help of Harry Houdini as she was working on cases that involved investment losses on the advice of mediums who claimed the ventures would be profitable. Houdini, impressed by her dedication and determination decided to show her the tricks that the supposed psychics were using in order to fool their clients into believing that their powers were genuine. Mackenberg began to work for Houdini as an investigator in 1925 as part of a team that would go undercover to various towns and cities to investigate mediums and spiritualists. To do this the team would often make visits to these groups under pseudonyms such as F. Raud (fraud) and using props such as walking sticks and hearing aids to see if anyone would question the use of them. The reason for this being is if the mediums were genuine, they would know that they had no use for these items. After Houdini's passing, Mackenberg continued her work into investigating and exposing fraudulent mediums by giving lectures in hopes of enlightening the public into how the scams worked.

- It is interesting to note that she was originally a believer in the paranormal in her early years but became more sceptical after her meeting with Houdini.

- Mackenberg was also one of Houdini's inner circle that was entrusted with a code word, that if spoken would prove that there was indeed an afterlife and that the person who gave the message may have genuine paranormal abilities. In 1945 Rose revealed she still had not received this message.

James 'The Amazing' Randi

James Randi, a name that struck fear into the heart of those who claimed to have paranormal abilities. Like Houdini, Randi was an accomplished magician and escape artist and once he retired, turned his attention and skills to uncovering the frauds and charlatans in the world of the paranormal. His first most famous case was that of Uri Geller. Geller gained fame for his claim of psychic powers which included telepathy, dowsing and Psychokinesiswhich allowed him to bend metal items such as spoons. Randi put forward the notion that Geller's power was nothing more than just illusion and magic tricks and showed how he himself could reproduce the same effects when using sleight of hand and some distraction techniques. A notable case of fraud that he did uncover was that of Peter Popoff. Popoff was an alleged faith healer in America in the 1980s. He seemed to have the supernatural ability to know the names of those in the audience and what afflicted them. How did he do it you ask? An investigation by Randi and a private investigator uncovered attendees filled out prayer cards in advance of the show and these were being read out by his wife directly to him through a transmission in his earpiece. Randi would go on to offer one million dollars to anyone who could prove under correct control conditions they could produce or prove they had some form of paranormal abilities. This prize remained unclaimed until it was officially disbanded in 2015. If you would like to know more about his career you should check out the documentary 'An Honest Liar.'

Derren Brown

Derren Brown is an English mentalist and illusionist, famous for his extravagant showmanship as featured in shows such as Russian Roulette, where live on air he quite literally dodged a bullet. In 2004 he undertook a project called Séance, in the program, he took twelve students from Rosehampton University to Elton Hall in East London, the site of an alleged mass suicide. Throughout the show Derren used techniques that were commonplace in spiritualism during the 1800s such as Ouija boards, automatic writing and a medium cabinet equipped with items such as a bell. A cabinet is a small unit surrounded by a curtain that a medium would enter in order to connect to the spirits. These items were used to create the feeling that the students were connecting to the spirit of Jane, one of the twelve students who committed suicide. At the end of the show, Derren revealed that Jane was in fact alive and well and the entire event that took place at the hall was entirely fictionalised and that he was able to create these illusions

132

through simple use of unconscious fraud and the ideomotor effect. In his 2005 special titled Messiah, Derren travelled to the United States to try and convince leading figures in different fields that he had a power that reflected that particular field. One of these powers was to be able to communicate with the dead. In this segment Brown explained how a claimed medium could just be using a technique called cold reading. During his séance he showed how effective this technique could be as he was able to convince three women that he was in contact with their loved ones. After the segment was complete, he explained to the audience that it was all a trick and that all the participants had agreed to the footage being broadcast. The important massage that Brown portrayed all the way through the show was that if at any point someone were to ask if he was a fake or a fraud, he would have told the truth. Another example of Derren using the cold reading was in the first episode of Derren Brown Investigates where he gave a reading to an actress from Hollyoaks. The results were quite interesting and one you should see for yourself.

Chapter Seventeen: Fraudulent Paranormal

'A closed mind is a dying mind'
Edna Ferber

The world of the paranormal field is a very interesting one however like most fields there are those out there who simply wish to take advantage of you be it for monetary or personal gain. In this chapter, I will discuss with you some of the techniques that these fraudsters could use in a hope to provide you some insight that would prevent you from not only being scammed but potentially protect you from emotionally hurt as well.

The rise of the spiritualist movement coincidently coincided with the rise of fraudulent practices taking place during séances that were nothing more than good illusions and magic tricks performed by alleged mediums. Some mediums at these séances claimed that they could produce a spiritual residue called ectoplasm. The mediums would only be able to produce this substance when the room was in total darkness and would stun those in attendance; however, on closer inspection these ectoplasm residues were nothing more than cheesecloth or textiles covered in potato starch giving the appearance that it was supernatural. Another example of this fraudulent activity can be found in the book Revelations of a Spirit Medium, Spiritualist myths exposed where the author reveals that spirit lights or ectoplasm could be produced simply by using a small, corked bottle filled with water and matchstick ends that once exposed to air would become luminous.

Cold reading is a technique that can be utilised by a reader to analyse a person's body language and expressions to dictate the correct statements to give. These statements are usually quite vague and are able to apply to most situations and people and are often referred to as Barnum statements. A Barnum statement is when a statement given by someone in this case, a 'medium' that could apply to a whole range of people because it is quite vague. An example of this technique would be 'You are a caring and generous person but sometimes you feel guilty that you can't do more.' Does this apply to you?

Hot reading is a technique where the reader has been given prior knowledge of the person, they are giving the reading to. With the advancement of modern technology hot reading has become much more prevalent and makes it much easier frauds to access personal information about you prior to a reading if you don't have the right privacy settings. A fraud could also use hot reading techniques in your own home, simply by being observant, looking at photographs, seeing if you are wearing a wedding ring. These hot reading techniques can be seen in the TV show Psych where the protagonist Shawn alludes to being a psychic but actually uses his photographic memory and his skill to notice the smallest details to help the police solve crimes.

In the world of the magicians there is a technique employed called mentalism. Mentalism is a performing art where the mentalist will use their senses to create the illusion of a Sixthsense to fool the audience that they have powers such as telepathy, clairvoyance and precognition. These same skills are what some sceptics claim fraudsters use to present mediumship abilities. A perfect example of this technique is shown in the TV series The Mentalist where the protagonist Jane used these techniques into fooling people into believing he was a medium.

Have you ever noticed that some of the most popular TV shows that are based around the paranormal always some with a 'This program is for entertainment purposes only' slogan? There is a very plausible reason for this. In 2005 TV show Most Haunted was reported to The Office of Communication in regard to 'techniques are used which means the audience is not necessarily in possession of the facts.' The ruling of OFCOM found in favour of Most Haunted ruling that 'It was not fraud as it was an entertainment show and was not a legitimate investigation into the paranormal and should not be taken seriously.' It is due to this ruling why most shows that investigate the paranormal now carry this warning.

It seems that the sensation for wanting to prove there is life after death can sometimes cloud our judgements, how so you ask? Just head over to well-known auction websites and type in 'haunted items' how many results did you find? As much as I would like to believe these items are truly haunted, the odds of this being so are quite low. It could be that the person who possessed the item is going through a tough time in their lives and associates this item with their bad luck, thus believing it is cursed or haunted. Then there is the other explanation, that it is all a scam. The reason I say this is because claiming that an item is haunted may peak a paranormal enthusiast interest to see if the item is haunted thus meaning that the seller can put a larger price tag on the said items. The interest in haunted items has always been around however interest in them has grown with paranormal shows such as Haunted Collector and Ghost Adventures, where its host Zak Bagans owns a haunted museum filled with haunted artefacts such as the Belagosi mirror and Jack Kevorkian's death van. Are these items you see for sale truly haunted? Who knows? All I can do is say 'buyer beware.'

Chapter Eighteen: Famous Paranormal Debunking

'Know the truth and the truth shall set you free'
Jesus Christ

There have been many famous paranormal claims that have been exposed as nothing more than a hoax. Is it for monetary gain, or an attempt to educate us into how we can be fooled? In this chapter, you will become more familiar with some of the most famous examples ever recorded and you can decide for yourself.

The Cottingley Fairies

In 1917 a series of photographs were taken by Elsie Wright and Frances Griffiths in which they can be seen playing with what appear to be fairies at the bottom of the Wrights' Garden. The photographs came to the attention of spiritualist Sir Arthur Conan Doyle who claimed that they were clear evidence of psychic phenomena. Doyle took the photographs to Kodak, where the images we expertly examined where it was proved that there was no sign of forgery made to the photo however, they stated it could not be taken as conclusive proof and refused to give the photo a certificate of authenticity. Doyle, in another attempt to verify the photographs presented them to Sir Oliver Lodge, a psychical researcher and physicist. Lodge suggested that he believed they were the product fraud and were indeed fakes. The story of the fairies finally saw a conclusion in the 1980s, when Elsie and Frances admitted that they were faked and were made using cardboard cut-outs from one of the children's books that they read at the time.

The Columbus Poltergeist

In 1984 there were reports taking place at the home of Tina Resch who seemed to be the focus of the haunting. This drew the attention of local news who took photographs of Tina while she was sat still in a chair that showed a telephone handset and phone cord flying in front of her. James Randi who worked with the Committee for Scientific Investigation of Claims of the Paranormal, was refused entry to investigate the case, but had suspected that Tina was faking the alleged paranormal activity. The case was proven to be a hoax when a visiting TV crew accidently left a camera recording which caught Tina knocking over a table lamp and screaming in fear. When confronted she claimed she did it so the reporters would leave.

The Sampford Poltergeist

This was a case that was reported in the early 1800s involved Mr John Chave and his family at Sampford Peverell. The house was allegedly by an entity during the day and at night with activity such as objects flying around the room and banging and rapping sounds. The case gained the interest of Reverend Caleb who wrote of his experiences claiming the activity to be genuine. It was eventually discovered however that the paranormal activity was probably the results of noises being created by smugglers who were behind a false wall which led to secret passages.

Project Alpha

In the 1970s magician and famous sceptic of the paranormal, James Randi contacted the McDonnell Laboratory for psychical research, offering suggestions on how to conduct their research in proper controlled conditions to help root out the fraudulent claimants. The offer was declined because of his reputation of being a showman rather than an unprejudiced critic. Unbeknownst to the laboratory, Randi had already begun to test the centre by placing two magicians, Steve Shaw and Mike Edwards, inside the laboratory in order to be tested for psychic abilities. Randi instructed the men that should they ever be asked if they are fake or faking activity, they should admit the truth. The two men were able to create great results until eventually the laboratory put tighter control measures in place. In 1983, Randi held a press conference where the deception of the project was revealed. The reaction to the reveal was mixed, with some critics calling the project's and Randi's ethics deplorable and would result in a setback for parapsychology research as a whole. Randi's supporters claim that it showed how truly flawed current research was and this experiment could be used to improve future research by using correct control measures.

The Carlos Hoax

The Carlos hoax was another attempt by James Randi to show how easily the public can be fooled into believing that paranormal activity is taking place when in fact it was nothing more than just good showmanship. In the 1980s the phenomenon known as 'channelling' was increasing in popularity. Channelling is where a spirit would possess and take over a host in order to express itself. Around the world thousands of people would attend shows to see people channelling so called spirits that would claim to be thousands of years old and often claiming to be important figures when they were alive. Randi decided to create a fictionalised spirit called Carlos that would possess a man called José Alvarez who would then proceed to use the techniques taught to him by Randi in order to put on a believable performance in Australia. To help sell the illusion Randi teamed up with Channel Nine Australia to help create a background, news articles and pamphlets to make the whole story seem legitimate. The news station even did an interview with José Alvarez who demonstrated his powers to them by making his pulse stop. The interview was a success and the illusion was sold, people were soon queuing to watch José Alvarez demonstrate his amazing powers at the Sydney Opera House. As Randi would point out, if at any point, there was anyone who was sceptical of the story, he would come clean. It would only require a small amount of research to reveal that his entire back story was indeed false and the publications that spoke of José Alvarez were fictional and never existed. Nobody ever questioned him.

The Fox Sisters

'I am here tonight as one of the founders of Spiritualism to denounce it as an absolute falsehood from beginning to end, as the flimsiest of superstitions, the most wicked blasphemy known to the world.' – Margaretta Fox Kane, New York World October 21st, 1888.

If you are familiar with the spiritualist movement, you will defiantly know about the Fox sisters. The sisters Catherine and Margaretta played a huge part in the creation of spiritualism starting in 1848. In 1848 the sisters allegedly made contact with a spirit by asking it to rap out their ages and even to answer yes or no questions depending on how many knocks were given. Through these rapping noises the 'spirit' was identified as a peddler called Charles B Rosna, however no person by that name was ever identified or reported missing. By 1850s the sisters had become a household name and were in high demand for their services and their séances. The popular theory put forward by scientists at the time was that the spirit rapping was nothing more than the cracking of joints. In 1851 three investigators from The University of Buffalo concluded that indeed the raps were created by the sisters cracking their lower joints and they showed this by placing a cushion under the sister's feet. After this was done the rapping's ceased. In 1857 The Boston Currier offered a reward of $500 price to anyone who could prove beyond the belief they could demonstrate paranormal abilities. The sisters tried and failed the challenge. Finally in 1888 Margaretta gave a confession to the New York World revealing how the sister's whole career was fraudulent and how they produced the noises. A year later she retracted her statement following pressure from the spiritualist movement, while this did not affect the movement as a whole the sister's credibility and career were in tatters, they died in poverty, shunned by their former supporters.

Spirit Photography

Spirit photography has one main goal in mind, to capture images of alleged spirit manifestations. Spirit photography has been the subject of many fraudulent claims since the invention of the camera. The most famous case of fraud is that of photographer William Mumler. Mumler discovered his photographs were showing signs of double exposure in 1862 when he took a self portrait of himself, when it was developed it showed the 'ghost' of his cousin who had died twelve years earlier. This discovery caused him to leave his job and take up spirit photography for which he gained quite a reputation which led him to work for some famous cliental including Abraham Lincolns wife Mary Todd

Lincoln. Eventually Mumler's deception was uncovered and was taken to court to be tried for fraud and larceny. Mumler was acquitted of all charges however, with the deception uncovered his career never recovered and he died in poverty.

Money for nothing

A strange title you may think however soon you will understand. Throughout the years there have been multiple cash challenges' out there for those who believe they have supernatural powers. The most famous was the million-dollar challenge offered by James Randi to anyone who could prove under controlled conditions could produce psychic activity. It has been recorded by the James Randi Educational Foundation that there were over one thousand applicants who had applied and failed up to the time when the challenge was terminated in 2015. The argument has been put forward by sceptics that because there are so many cash challenges out there, why with all the claims of paranormal activity do the majority of prizes go unclaimed? The answer, because under strict conditions no true paranormal evidence can be produced.

Chapter Nineteen: Glossary of Paranormal Terms

'The beautiful thing about learning is nobody can take it
away from you'
B. B. King

- Alfie Kalts: Anagram of 'it's all fake'

- Backscatter: Optical phenomena resulting in balls of
  light appearing in photographs.

- Barnum Statement: A vague statement that can apply
  to multiple people.

- Cold Reading: Statements allegedly gained by
  paranormal means but are just vaguely accurate
  statements that could apply to anyone.

- Cursed Artefact: An item that has a negative
  association attributed to it.

- Debunk: Attempts to find logical explanations for
  paranormal activity.

- Demon: A supernatural entity typically associated
  with evil.

- Divination: The attempt to gain insight into a
  question or situation by supernatural means.

- Dowsing: The use of rods to locate water, metal or precious minerals.

- Ectoplasm: Substance believed to be left behind by a ghostly encounter

- Elemental: An elemental is a term used to describe an entity that was neither human nor demonic and is often associated with the practice of witchcraft.

- EMF: Electromagnetic Fluctuation, ghosts are believed to be able to manipulate this type of energy.

- ESP: Extra sensory perception, a general term to define all psychic abilities.

- EVP: Electronic Voice Phenomena. Voices that weren't heard until a playback of the recording.

- Fran Tudule: Anagram of 'Fraudulent'

- Ghost: Term commonly used to describe the spirit of a deceased person.

- Haunted Artefact: An item allegedly imbued with a spirit.

- Hot reading: A technique where the reader has been given prior knowledge of the person, they are giving the reading to.

- Ideomotor effect: psychological phenomena where a person makes motions unconsciously.

- Incubus: A demon in the form of a male who lies with sleeping women in order to engage in sexual activity.

- Medium: An individual who can see, speak or feel spirit entities.

- Mentalism: A Practice of simulating ESP such as telepathy.

- Muscle movements: A phenomena that mimics telepathy in which a person is able to interpret unconscious muscular movements.

- Orbs: Believed to be the first stage of a spiritual manifestation or the result of backscatter.

- Ouija Board: Also known as a talking board, a device marketed as a toy that some believe can be used to contact the dead.

- Paranormal: Describes events that are beyond the scope of normal scientific understanding.

147

- Paranormal Investigator: An individual who specialises in paranormal phenomena such as hauntings.

- Parapsychologist: An individual who specialises in investigating and testing claims of psychic phenomena.

- Parapsychology: a study into the unexplained, it is considered a pseudoscience.

- Pareidolia: The tendency to incorrectly perceive what an object or pattern is. To see human/animal features in random shapes.

- Pendulum: A weight hung from a fixed point so that it is able to swing freely.

- Poltergeist: From the German words 'poltern' meaning noisy and 'geist' meaning ghost.

- Possession: When a spirit or entity is able to overtake an individual's body and personality with or without permission.

- Pseudoscience: statements of beliefs, or practices that claim to be both scientific and factual but are incompatible with the scientific methodology.

- Rob Suttellock: Anagram of 'utter bollocks'

- Sceptic: An individual who requires definitive proof of the paranormal and seeks out logical explanations for paranormal activity.

- Séance: Old French word for session, group sessions held in order to attempt communication with the spirit world.

- Spiritualism: A religious movement that hold the belief that spirits of the dead exist and can communicate with the living.

- Succubus: A demon that appears in a female form to seduce men in their dreams.

- Trigger Objects: Physical objects such as crosses that are used to see if spirits will interact with them.

- UFO: Unidentified Flying Object

- Zener Cards: A set of 25 cards that are used to test for ESP

Chapter Twenty: Final Thought

'May the paranormal road lead you to truth; seek the
truth not the hunt'
Shea

If you have made it this far, I would like to say thank you. This was my first attempt at writing a book and many hours of research has gone into trying to make it an insightful one. I have tried to be open minded while writing the book, maybe I have made you a believer? Or maybe even a believer into a sceptic? That is the true beauty of this book, it is all down to how you want to view the paranormal. To those who are interested in the parapsychology I will say there are many ways you can take up the subject. The University of Edinburgh offers perhaps the best insight as you can undertake a degree in the subject, if you are a student of psychology. There are also courses available online that you can take to broaden your knowledge and understanding of the subject, just be sure to check that the course and the provider are officially recognised by a genuine awarding body. Be sure to check out the bibliography section where I have recommended some knowledgeable books on the subject. To those interested in becoming a paranormal investigator, perhaps you are thinking of forming your own team? Just remember this hobby doesn't come cheap and you won't always get the results you want. I would highly recommend that you should check if there are any paranormal teams recruiting, this way you gain practical and first-hand knowledge. Finally to those who are thinking of visiting a medium for a reading always keep an open mind and give as little away as possible. In no way am I saying there are not genuine mediums out there but there are those who will just try to take advantage of you.

Bibliography, Source Materials and Useful Websites

- Centre Of Excellence Parapsychology course module 1, Chapter 3: Glossary of Terms

- Derren Brown Trick of the mind (and any of his TV specials)

- Encyclopaedia of frauds and hoaxes of the occult and supernatural by James Randi

- Field guide to Ghost Hunting Techniques by Dale Kaczmarek

- Ghostwatch: The BBC spoof that fooled a nation – a BBC news article

- Ghost And the Paranormal published by igloobooks

- Guidelines for testing psychic claimants by Richard Wiseman and Robert L. Morris

- Haunted Sheffield by Mr & Mrs P Dreadful

- Parapsychology by Caroline Watt

- Parapsychology The controversial science by Richard Broughton

- Science & Séance by Ciaran O'Keeffe& Billy Roberts

- The Element Encyclopaedia of The Psychic World by Teresa Cheung

- The Element Encyclopaedia of Secret Signs and Symbols by Adele Nozedar

- The Element Encyclopaedia of Ghost and Hauntings by Teresa Cheung

- The Ghost Hunters guide: Illustrated Edition by Peter Underwood

- Wikipedia (various articles)

- https://www.atlasobscura.com/articles/in-1926-houdini-spent-4-days-shaming-congress-for-being-in-thrall-to-fortunetellers

- https://amityvillemurders.com/the-haunting/the-true-story-of-112-ocean-avenue.html

- https://www.conandoyleinfo.com/life-conan-doyle/conan-doyle-and-spiritualism/

- https://darkhauntings.wordpress.com

- https://www.history.com/topics/religion/buddhism#:~:t
ext=Buddhism%20is%20a%20faith%20that,of%20the%20
major%20world%20religions.

- http://leapcastle.net/

- www.mentalfloss.com

- https://www.scoopwhoop.com/culture/cursed-items-
from-around-the-world/

- https://www.spr.ac.uk/

- https://www.walksofitaly.com/blog/art-culture/paris-
catacombs

Printed in Great Britain
by Amazon